I0475011

Dirty Little Secrets

Copyright © 2013 Dr. Carlyle W. Rogers III
All rights reserved.

ISBN: 1452813094
ISBN-13: 9781452813097

Library of Congress Control Number: 2010905533
CreateSpace Independent Publishing Platform,
North Charleston, SC

Dirty Little Secrets: Declassifying the Employment Game

Dr. Carlyle W. Rogers III

Acknowledgements

First and foremost, I want to thank the countless employees, colleagues, managers, executives, business professionals, and friends who demonstrated an endless supply of positives, negatives, wins, losses, successes, and failures in the workplace over the past 23 years. It has only been through these experiences that I was able to write this book.

I also want to send a big thanks to my little brother, Christopher Rogers, for lending his time and expertise to edit my first book. On top of being a husband, dad, artist, and author, he managed to fit in time for his big brother.

Finally, I want to thank my daughter, Mya Rogers, for inspiring me to be the best I can be, teaching me patience, and reminding about the importance of maintaining a good sense of humor. I love you pumpkin and hope that this book will inspire you to do great things in your future.

Table of Contents

Chapter 1: Introduction
Using This Book... 1
What You Don't Know Can Hurt You.............................. 2

Chapter 2: The Pre-Employment Phase
Finding the Jobs.. 7
Online Job Boards 9
Temporary Agencies and Recruiters 10
Job Applications.. 12
Resumes 14
Introduction to Interviewing 17
Types of Questions to Expect in an Interview.............. 20
Preparing for the Interview.. 22
Compensation... 24
Negotiating Salaries 28
References 30
Background Checks... 32
Pre-Employment Assessments 35
Drug Testing 36
Job Offers 37

Chapter 3: The Employment Phase
The New Hire Process 41
Employee Paperwork 45
The Employee Handbook 45
Payroll... 47
Employee Benefits 49
Paid Time Off.. 55
Leaves of Absence 56
Disciplinary Actions 58
Corporate Structure 61

Corporate Departments...64
Dealing with Politics..65
Sexual Harassment...67
Discrimination 69
Training 71
Dating in the Workplace 72
Workplace Injuries and Illnesses 73
Disabilities/Disabling Conditions 75
Miscellaneous Things to Know 79
Termination of Employment..83

Chapter 4: The Post-Employment Phase
Surviving Unemployment..87
What Happens to Your Health Coverage 88
Unemployment Benefits 91
Wrongful Termination...94

Chapter 5: Resources
Federal Labor and Employment Agencies.......................97
State Employment and Labor Agencies 99
Family and Medical Leave Act 101
Americans with Disabilities Act
Amendments Act 104
Civil Rights Act of 1964 and Title VII 105
Age Discrimination in Employment Act of 1967.........106
Genetic Information Nondiscrimination Act 108
Resources for Military Reservists 109
List of Popular Recruiting & Temporary Agencies 112
List of Commonly Used Online Job Boards..................113

Preface

A couple of years ago I began to reflect upon my life and career. One of the fundamental concepts I kept coming back to was how fortunate I had been to receive such great exposure to a variety of cultures, philosophies, beliefs, practices, and of course...people.

Fast forward 23 years... I had accomplished a great deal of education, obtained a great deal of business experience, had been the chief people and strategic advisor to numerous Presidents and CEOs, had experienced and observed an endless supply of successes and failures, and watched kids (who were born after I graduated from high school) enter the workforce. Beyond being a reminder of how quickly time passes, I realized that I had been in a very unique position making me privy to both sides of corporate life as well as the respective impact upon people and decision making. At any given time, my role required that I be the balance, the listener, the glue, the decision maker, the spin-master, the politician, the instigator, the manipulator, the good-guy, and the bad-guy. This subsequently placed me in a position to create, observe, direct, manipulate, shift, and manage the balance between management and non-management (or for many, us and them).

Having been the head of corporate human resources departments, assisting and coaching countless senior executives with decision making, and being directly involved in making key and critical corporate business decisions for so long, I began to recognize a consistent theme amongst employees, regardless of company, city, state, or country. This consistency was a serious degree of misunderstanding, misinformation, inaccurate beliefs, insecurity, and information that was situated to set them up for failure in the workplace. I realized that I had to do something. Thus, Dirty Little Secrets was born.

Dirty Little Secrets is not intended to be a cheat sheet for employees, but to be a guide for becoming and being a successful employee. I have attempted to capture the topics that I have experienced the most as well as have included information that is often believed to be true... but has not been articulated well. Specifically, information about the realities of how and why decisions are made in the workplace... without placing a politically correct spin on it.

I also hope that members of management realize the importance of the information presented in the book. Although it clearly is a road map for employees, it is also a great developmental tool for managers. Savvy managers will quickly identify that it is also a road map for helping them become more successful managers by avoiding the pitfalls and recognizing the opportunities.

In closing, in an effort to ensure an easy read, I choose to format the book as headings with quick bullet points. I have come to realize that most business books are quite obnoxious to read, thus often being overlooked by the average employee or member of management. This is a shame as many of those books possess quality information. If the authors had taken a quick moment to recognize that employees typically don't even take the time to read their employee handbooks, they may have chosen a format better suited for the audience. It is important to note that there is no particular order for the bullet points; therefore the order does not signify importance.

It is also very important to understand that the book is written from a general perspective for most topics and federal perspective related to employment laws. Thus, keep in mind that employment laws and practices are always changing, being revised, being clarified, and so on. It is also extremely important to recognize that it is written from a non-union, non-collective-bargaining perspective (as these environments are subject to contracts and the practices vary). If you have questions about how a specific law or practice applies to your state, please be sure to seek out the respective employment agency to clarify the current laws and practices (see Chapter 5 for a list of state employment agencies).

Please enjoy and I hope that it provides you with the information that you need to be successful in your employment.

Carlyle Rogers

Dr. Carlyle W. Rogers

Chapter 1: Introduction

Using This Book

Congratulations! You have taken a significant step towards becoming employed and becoming a successful employee. At a minimum, when you finish reading this book, you will have a much better understanding of the common practices and philosophies related to workplace environments…thus empowering you to make better decisions.

In light of this, it is also important to understand that with this knowledge comes accountability. Regardless of any resources, information or guidance that you receive about a topic, unless you apply yourself and accept the results, it is waste of time and energy.

Although it may seem cynical or pessimistic as you read certain sections, this book is not intended to be interpreted as such. It is meant to cut through the illusions, spin, smoke and mirrors. **Only when you recognize the realities of the workplace can you truly become a successful employee.**

<u>Tips</u>

- Remember that this is a guide. Workplace environments, practices, employment laws, and cultures vary.

- Remember that the information is intended to educate, stimulate thought, and prepare you for situations, events and topics that you may encounter in the workplace. It is not intended to be interpreted or accepted as the sole guide to all workplaces and subsequent decisions that you may make.

- Your company human resources department (if it has one) is usually a great place to start when you have questions related to company culture, policies and practices.

- Your company may or may not have resources reflecting practices, policies, procedures, and expectations. If these resources aren't made readily available to you, ask for them. These may include Employee Handbooks, Policy and Procedure Manuals, and training materials.

- Local, state and federal employment and labor laws are always subject to change, modification, revision, and amending. The references to specific laws contained in this book are based upon current information at the time of writing. Please be sure to refer to the specific agencies or legal entities responsible for those laws and practices to obtain additional clarity and possible changes that may impact their application.

- If you have questions related to how any information in this book may apply to your specific federal or state employment and labor laws, it is always recommended that you seek qualified legal counsel (a.k.a. "employment or labor lawyer") to confirm.

What You Don't Know Can Hurt You

*One of the lessons in life that I believe has an application to just about anything you do is that "knowledge is power". Whether getting married, having children, driving a car, picking a vacation destination, or being an employee...**the more that you know about the specific topic, the more likely you will be to succeed.***

<u>Tips</u>

- You know the old saying, if you assume you make "an ass out of u and me" (ass u me). Don't ever forget this!

- All employers are different. Just because things happened one way in a previous job doesn't mean they will happen the same way in your new job.

- Most employers are interested in only one thing... profitability. This doesn't mean they don't care about you (or does it?)

- To most employers, employees are either indispensable or dispensable. Which one will you strive to be?

- There is a good chance that your manager has never had management training.

- Managers tend to fall into four main categories...

  a. ***Managementus Unlimitus Supplius***: Poor job skills AND poor people management skills (most likely to experience in the workplace)
  b. ***Managementus Maximus Perfomancus***: Good job skills AND poor people management skills (these are the people promoted into management because they were good performers in their previous roles)
  c. ***Managementus Happieus Peoplus***: Poor job skills AND good people management skills
  d. ***Managementus Rarous***: Good job skills AND good people management skills (least likely to experience in the workplace)

- There is a good chance that you will not be adequately trained to do your job. Your success will often be tied to your personal initiative.

- How one person perceives a work environment, co-worker or manager will likely be different than how you will perceive that same environment, co-worker or manager. The bottom line…draw your own conclusions based upon your experience, interactions, and observations.

- Although skill and performance are important, who you know and how well you play the game play a significant role in your career.

- Decisions and actions in the workplace are not always logical, ethical, rational, or legal.

- You may be absolutely right about something, but that doesn't mean that it will happen or be accepted by your manager.

- Your manager or someone higher up the management chain is usually going to make the final decision. You may or may not agree with or like it and may or may not have an opportunity to influence the decisions.

- Business is not about being fair. Don't get hung up on this philosophy.

- There are individuals in the organization that have significant influence on key decision makers. Like it or not, it is politically smart to keep them close.

- Management, competence and accountability do not always coexist in the workplace.

- Regardless of what they will tell you, an "ivory tower" is usually in effect when it comes to senior and executive management.

- You are responsible for how you behave, respond, work, and perform in the workplace. Although others may influence any of the above, you have the ultimate ability to decide.

- The hardest working and best performing employees aren't always the ones promoted and recognized. Like it or not, it is often a game of favorites.

- A frustrating element for senior management is when employees do not have an understanding of the costs of doing business. Just because a company makes money doesn't mean that it has endless supplies of money available for employees and programs.

- Chances are you will not be the only employee in a company. Learn quickly that it is not all about you and everything that happens impacts the entire organization.

- There is often not a lot of love between operations and support functions (i.e., human resources, marketing, finance, etc.). This is most often due to short sightedness and ignorance as both sides play important roles in the success or failure of the organization.

Chapter 2: The Pre-Employment Phase

Finding the Jobs

In essence, the less effort that you put into your job search, the more likely you are to fail. **When seeking employment, you had better approach it as a full-time job!**

<u>Tips</u>

- Be prepared to commit a lot of time to the job search process. This means time each day… and possibly to months of searching.

- Exhaust as many resources as possible. Technology has been generous to the employment seeking market as it provides access to countless job search resources.

- Look into online job boards, newspapers, local publications (i.e., newspapers), your local chamber of commerce, local temporary agencies, recruiting firms, state unemployment agencies, churches and local businesses for job posting and opportunities.

- Use other online resources, such as social and business related sites. These may include such sites as Facebook, LinkedIn, and Twitter. Make an announcement that you are pursuing new work and specify the types of jobs if possible. One of your friends or contacts just may know of an opportunity that is not posted or advertised.

- Research companies in your area. The Chamber of Commerce is a great place to start. Go directly to the company website to see what opportunities have been posted. Some employers do not advertise beyond their company website.

- Friends and family are also great resources for jobs as they can provide inside information about the companies they work for.

- Be realistic in your search. If you are new to the workforce, it is probably not reasonable to seek out President/CEO roles. Applying to jobs that you are not qualified for will only reduce your chances for securing employment.

- Realize that job searches can take time. Many events influence markets, thus affecting job creation, availability and internal hiring practices in your field of expertise.

- If you are currently attending college, see if they offer career placement assistance or job boards.

- Attend local job fairs. You can often find these at schools, universities, and in publications.

- Know what you are looking for. If you are entering the job market or considering a career change, take time to review job descriptions, job postings, and occupational outlooks to understand required skills, education, training, earnings, and opportunities.

Online Job Boards and Recruiting

One of the best things that could ever have happened to job searching is the internet. The internet provides vast options for researching companies and looking for work. The biggest challenge with the internet, however, is time. **Be prepared to invest a substantial amount of time surfing the web, reading job descriptions, filling out online applications, and investigating opportunities.**

<u>Tips</u>

- Block off as much time as possible to use the internet for your job search. The great news is that it is available 24 hours a day, 7 days a week.

- If you have a smart phone, look for job search engines that have mobile sites to keep you up-to-date when you are on the go.

- Be prepared to have to complete detailed information about your past work experience and education.

- Have an electronic copy of your resume, cover letter, and compensation history ready to load onto job search sites.

- If possible, have electronic copies of college transcripts, professional references, letters of recommendation and work related training certificates available to load onto job search sites. Certain employers require this information when applying for jobs online.

- Have employment addresses, dates of employment, supervisor's names and phone numbers, earnings history, and college/university addresses readily available.

- Some employers and recruiters only use certain job sites. If you limit your information to one or two sites, your resume may not be found. The more visible you are the more likely you are to be discovered. **Post your information on as many job search sites as possible.**

- Many employers have company applicant tracking systems that link to various recruiting sites. Be sure to complete all of the requested information and follow directions.

- Refresh your resume every two to three weeks on each job board. As time goes on, more resumes are posted to these boards. Yours moves to the bottom of the list.

- A sample listing of commonly used online job boards can be found in Chapter 5.

- If an employer asks for compensation history and required salary, provide it. Many times recruiters will pass on candidates that do not provide this information. Also, it assists with wasting yours and the company's time if your requirements aren't consistent with what they have budgeted to pay.

- If the advertisement doesn't specify that you need to contact the company directly...don't. There is nothing more annoying to recruiters than people who can't follow directions.

Temporary Agencies and Recruiters

Temporary agencies and recruiting firms are great places to gain assistance with your job search. These two types of companies are in the business of finding jobs for job seeker, while employers rely upon them to fill their temporary, part-time, full-time and contract labor needs. **Temporary agencies and recruiting firms often have the inside track to your next career.**

Tips

- A great way to find local temporary agencies is to go to your phone book or search online. Some temporary agencies are part of large national chains while others are local or regional. Please refer the Appendix for a list of some well-known temporary agencies.

- When applying at a temporary agency, be prepared to set aside a couple of hours for interviews and testing. It is not uncommon to have your computer application skills assessed (i.e., MS Word, Excel, PowerPoint, Outlook, etc.).

- Temporary agencies often require you to call in every morning that you are available to work (for temporary assignments). Be prepared every morning to have an opportunity to work. This means getting out of bed early, eating breakfast and having your work attire ready to go.

- There are countless recruiting firms ranging from sole proprietorships to national chains. Some provide job or industry specific services while others do not. The best way to search for recruiting firms is online or via word of mouth. Please refer to the Appendix for a list of some well-known recruiting firms.

- Be wary of recruiters who want to charge you to assist with your job search. I usually recommend against paying anyone to find you a job. The common practice is that recruiters are paid by the client (the employer) on a contingency or retainer basis. Chances are if you are asked to pay the recruiter, you are being scammed, wasting your time, and wasting your money.

- You may or may not be required to meet with the recruiting firm in person. Many recruiters are independent and work via phone, email and internet. Others may require a brief meeting to get an idea of how you present yourself before they submit you to their client or an employer.

- Be patient with recruiters. They tend to be temperamental and will contact you when they are ready. This is a place where persistence may not be a successful approach.

- Recruiters are not usually personable, are up against deadlines, under a lot of pressure from their clients, and interested in securing the deal, as this is how they get paid. Don't be offended if they seem distant or are not chatty.

Job Applications

For many, the application process may be the beginning and end of their employment journey. Most often, entry level, line, retail, hospitality, service, restaurant and related jobs require that an applicant complete a short, or sometimes lengthy, document requesting information about their experience, education and references. It is at this point that a recruiter or hiring manager often makes a decision whether or not they will consider you to be a viable candidate. **Therefore, it is critical that you understand the application before beginning.**

<u>Tips</u>

- When you get an application, take a moment to read through the entire document before you begin filling it out.

- Use a blue or black ink pen.

- Be sure to write legibly.

- Be prepared to provide detailed information related to your work experience and education. For instance:

  a. Name, address and phone number of company/school
  b. Your title and job responsibilities in previous jobs
  c. Your manager's name and phone number
  d. How much you made at your previous jobs (wage or salary)
  e. Why you left your previous employer
  f. Degrees, diplomas, etc. earned from school

- Be sure that you complete every field in the application. If it does not apply, then place "N/A" in the blank to reflect "not applicable".

- Do not omit information. This is typically viewed as lying via concealing or lack of attention to detail.

- Provide only truthful responses. Falsifying information (a.k.a. "lying") guarantees that your application will be passed over or that you will be fired at a later time when the deception has been discovered.

- Be sure to initial all places that require your initials.

- Be sure to sign all places that require your signature.

- Proofread the application before submitting it.

- Certain questions that should never be asked by a potential employer on an application (pre-hire) or in a pre-employment interview include:

  a. How old are you or what is your date of birth?
  b. When did you graduate from high school or college?
  c. Are you married?
  d. Do you have children?
  e. What is your sexual orientation (straight, homosexual, bisexual, etc.)?
  f. What is your religion?
  g. Are you pregnant (or how far along are you)?
  h. What country are you from?
  i. Are you a US Citizen?

Resumes

*This is the one opportunity you will have to convince a recruiter or hiring manager that you are worth talking to. **Think of your resume as the quickest 10 seconds you will ever have to sell yourself.***

<u>Tips</u>

- Although there are countless numbers of people trying to convince you to purchase their resume writing format, the reality is that there is no single accepted or proper format for a resume.

- Some resumes are one-pagers and some are more. The length of the resume will likely be determined by your experience. If it appears that you are going to exceed 2 pages…take a moment to review it to ensure that you limit it to what is really necessary.

- Read the job description for the job you are trying to get. This will cue you in to the items you will need to be sure to include in your resume, assuming that you possess those skills and qualifications.

- The three main fields that you need to include in your resume are contact information (name, address, phone numbers, and email address), work experience and education.

- Other common fields include job objective, skills, accomplishments and professional organizations that you belong to.

- In the United States, you should not include such items as your age, marital status, whether or not you have children, veteran status, disabling conditions, photos, religious affiliations, sexual preferences, or dates you graduated from high school or college.

- If you have little or no work experience, a recommended and common order of sections on your resume may include the following: Objective, Skills, Education, Work Experience

- If you have experience, a recommended and common order of sections on your resumes may include the following: Objective, Skills, Work Experience, Education

- In the "Experience" section of your resume, be sure to include your accomplishments. For instance, "increased sales from $100,000 to $500,000", "improved customer service levels", "saved the company $50,000 by reducing employee turnover", "managed 50 employees", or "improved customer service". This is your chance to shine and get the hiring manager or recruiter's attention.

- When listing Education and Experience, place them in chronological order. The most commonly used approach is the most recent job first (for Experience) and first education earned first (for Education). For example:

Experience

➢	ABC Employer	Manager	Jan 2007 to Present
➢	DEF Employer	Supervisor	Jan 2001 to Dec 2006
➢	GHI Employer	Lead	Jan 1990 to Dec 2000

Education

➢	High School Diploma	ABC High School
➢	Bachelor's Degree, Psychology	DEF University
➢	Master of Business Administration	GHI University

Keep in mind:

- Proofread your resume before you submit it to anyone! If possible, have someone else take a look to check for errors in punctuation, clarity and readability.

- Employers and recruiters do not tend to care about your hobbies. This is an outdated concept and should not be included on your resume.

- The person reading your resume may or may not have experience reading a resume.

- You have an average of 5 to 10 seconds to gain the attention of the person reading the resume. Be sure to have your key applicable skills and experience jumping off the page.

Introduction to Interviewing

Although there are a handful of commonly practiced styles of interviewing, you never know what you will be up against. The best thing you can do is have a good understanding of the common types of interviews conducted and realize that the person interviewing you is just a person. Moreover, the interviewer may have no experience interviewing or with the interview process. **Best advice, be prepared for anything!**

Tips

- Like it or not, interviews are often subject to the interviewers experience, personal biases, beliefs and values.

- Although not a legal practice, discrimination against candidates based upon factors such as race, age, gender, pregnancy, disability, etc., is more common than you think.

- Factors that tend to be used against candidates are their history of litigation against a former employers and history of workers compensation (being injured on the job and filing subsequent claims). Note: Whether legal or not, this happens.

- Your fate can often be determined within the first 30 seconds of when the interviewer sees you.

- You would be amazed how many interviewers immediately reject candidates based upon their height, weight, fashion or perceived attractiveness.

- If you are rejected based upon any of the above examples, don't expect to be told that you were rejected based upon those criteria.

- The most common types of interviews include unstructured (anything goes), behavioral (probative), competency-based (company/candidate qualities matching), and panel (multiple interviewers at one time).

- Unstructured interviews are not predictable. Questions may include basic questions (closed-ended/yes-no) to soliciting detailed information (open-ended).

- One belief is that past behaviors predict future behaviors. Behavioral interviewing will challenge your actual experience. The interviewer seeks to discover whether or not you have actual, theoretical, or no experience in specific areas.

- Seasoned interviewers using a behavioral interviewing approach will likely continue to ask more detailed questions based upon your answers. This provides excellent insight into your practical knowledge of a topic. For example:

  a. Give me an example of when you had to plan and manage a project.
  b. Give me an example of how you used other departments to assist with the completion of the project.
  c. Give me an example of when you were not able to complete a project on time.

     d. How did you address the lack of timely delivery of the results?

- Competency-based interviews are an attempt to determine if you match core skill sets the company employees share.

- Panel interviews may seem daunting, but do not fear. Just because there are multiple people in the room doesn't mean this is a time to stress. Just relax, take your time and do your best.

- Arrive to your interview 10 minutes before you are scheduled to be there. Never be late!

- Don't be afraid of the interviewers. Although many interviewers like to come across as tough, they are people too.

- Interviews should be two-sided. Make a list of questions to ask the interviewer. Be sure they are work/company related. Both you and the interviewer should use this time to discover if there is a good fit.

- Never enter an interview without information about the company and what it does. If they have a website, visit it. Research and prepare.

- Listen closely to the interviewer. If you are unsure about a question or something stated, ask the interviewer to clarify.

- Speak slowly and articulate. When people are interviewing, it is not uncommon for them to be nervous.

- Be prepared to discuss any gaps in your employment history.

Types of Questions to Expect in an Interview

The only guarantee that you will ever have with interviewing questions is that you never know what you will encounter. ***The best weapons that you will have against uncertainty will be having a solid understanding of common interviewing styles and knowledge of the questions typically asked in an interview.***

Tips

- Questions directly tied to information provided in your resume or application. If you provide it…you had better be ready to explain it in detail.

- Yes-No Questions (aka "closed-ended" questions) require a simple yes or no response. For instance:

    a. Did you graduate from high school?
    b. Have you ever been fired from a job?
    c. Have you ever been disciplined at work?
    d. Have you ever lied on an application?
    e. Have you ever stolen from an employer?
    f. Have you ever used a cash register?
    g. Have you ever managed or supervised employees?
    h. Do you have experience doing…(fill in job specific skills)?
    i. Have you ever written a schedule?
    j. Have you ever worked for us before?
    k. Do you work well with other people?

- Fact-Finding or Validating Questions are used to gain basic responses and information from the candidate. For instance:

  a. When did you work at ABC employer?
  b. Why did you leave your last job?
  c. What were your responsibilities in your job?
  d. What are your three best qualities?
  e. What are three areas that you need to develop (sometimes posed as "weaknesses)?
  f. What did you like best or least about your last job?
  g. What did you like best or least about your last supervisor?
  h. Why are you interested in working here?
  i. What do you know about our company?

- Open-Ended Questions are designed to gain in depth information about what you really do or don't know.

For instance:

  a. Tell me about a time when you…
     …*dealt with an unhappy customer*
  b. How did you handle the matter?
  c. Give me an example of when you were unable to satisfy the customer.
  d. Give me an example of when you were able to satisfy the customer.
     …*were unable to meet a deadline*
     …*completed a project before its deadline*
     …*had to manage a multi-department project*
  e. Give me an example of when you were unable to influence a supervisor.
  f. Tell me how you dealt with…

...a conflict between two employees.
...a customer escalation.
g.   Give me an example of when...
...you had to manage a project
...you planned an event
...you trained employees how to (fill in the blank with job specific skills).

Preparing for the Interview

If you have ever heard the expression "you only get one chance to make a first impression", an interview is the moment that is referenced. This is the time when you and the employer will examine each other and determine if there is a fit...not necessarily a skill fit...but will you be able to work together. **An interview is your opportunity to shine.**

<u>Tips</u>

- Research the company. Know their business.

- Read the job description for the position you are interviewing for. This provides insight into the skills being sought by the employer.

- Get adequate sleep the night before your interview.

- If you don't have G.P.S in your car, be sure to find directions to the interviewing site the day before your interview.

- Eat a light meal before your interview.

- Dress for success! Take a shower, wear clean and pressed clothes, and don't overdo your make-up, accessories, cologne or perfume. Check yourself in the mirror before you leave.

- Bring at least 5 copies of your resume (if you have one) to the interview. Print resumes on plain, white paper. Colored paper is annoying and is often difficult to photocopy.

- If the company sent you homework or assessments to complete, be sure they are done and that you have the assignments with you.

- Have a list of questions you want to ask the interviewer prepared in advance. This shows that you are interested.

- Bring a notebook and pen so that you can take notes or jot down questions that may come to mind during the interview. This lets the interviewer know that you are listening.

- Do not ever be late! Arrive 10 minutes early to the interviewing site. Showing up too early can also be viewed as a mistake.

- Your interview starts at the door. Be sure to greet the receptionist when you arrive. Remember that these critical moments have caused countless candidates to be rejected because they were ill-mannered when they arrived.

- When your interviewer arrives, be sure to greet them with a handshake and smile. Introduce yourself using your first and last name.

- Once you arrive in the office or location you will be interviewing, RELAX and BREATHE!!!

- Take your seat. Use good posture, sit up straight and listen closely to the interviewer.

- Take your time when answering questions. Speak slowly and clearly.

- If you do not know the answer to a question or lack the skills and experience requested, be sure to respond accordingly. Don't try to fake your way through it. Deception will most likely backfire on you later in the interview process.

- Stay focused and do not stray off course. Although it is easy to want to find common ground or discuss non-work related topics with the interviewer, this is a disastrous approach often taught by interviewing instructors that can quickly backfire if the candidate does not understand where to set boundaries. Although the interviewer may engage the conversation, they will be assessing your ability to stay on task.

- When the interview is over, be sure to thank the interviewer for their time and shake the interviewer's hand.

Compensation

Compensation (a.k.a. "salary" or "wages") is the term that refers to the money you will receive for working. This may be an hourly wage or annual salary. It may also include such things as a bonus, commission, equity (i.e., stock), and other incentives.

Tips

- Compensation is a broad term. Typically, it refers to base wages whether hourly or salary, bonuses, commissions, equity (i.e., shares, options), and incentives.

- Salaries are most often influenced by a variety of factors including the geography or location where you will be working, annual revenues or how much money the company makes in a year, the number of employees in the company, and the industry the business is in (i.e., manufacturing, services, aerospace, healthcare, etc.).

- Be cautious about relying upon online salary calculators as your experience, education, skills and earnings history may not warrant the reflected range that you find.

- When employers think of compensation, it is usually associated with a number that includes what they pay you over the course of the year, the amount's they pay for your benefits and taxes they pay related to your pay and employment. When approaching compensation, let's imagine you earn $50,000 per year, and the employer pays for 75% of your employee benefits (medical and dental).

   Your total compensation package may look something like this:

   a. $50,000 for salary
   b. $2,700 for benefits (75% of $300 for 12 months)
   c. $6,000 for taxes
   d.   Your total compensation is actually about $58,700

e. A quick note to understand a large piece of an employer's cost's just to pay employees to stay in business…

Imagine a company has 500 employees with each averaging $50,000 salary per year with benefits. The cost just to pay employees…nothing related to conducting business itself (i.e., infrastructure, products, supplies, etc.)…would be around $29,350,000 (29 million dollars).

- A salary is usually based upon a 12 month period of time (annual salary). This is usually a fixed number (i.e., $50,000 per year). Employees who receive a set salary are usually not entitled to overtime pay (see "exempt vs. non-exempt employees").

- An hourly wage is a set amount that is paid for each hour worked. Unlike a salary, the amount an employee may earn is tied to the number of hours that they work. These employees are typically entitled to receive overtime pay, depending upon the state for overtime payment rules.

    For example, Employee A earns $10 per hour. Week 1 they work 40 hours and earn $400 (gross…before taxes). Week 2 they work 25 hours and earn $250 (gross…before taxes).

- Non-discretionary (tied to a plan) bonuses are typically provided to exempt (salaried) employees and/or executives. It is not as common for hourly employees to receive a non-discretionary bonus.

- Bonus plans vary on their administration and are commonly paid on an annual basis.

- It is common that bonus plans will be tied to **MBOs** or Management by Objectives...which effectively means goals or objectives to meet...and/or company performance (revenues, EBITDA, OIBA, profit, etc.).

- It is common for bonuses to be a percentage of an annual salary. These percentages are often associated with the level of role. For instance:

  Employee A is a manager and is eligible to earn 10% of their annual salary. Employee A makes $50,000 per year and therefore is entitled to earn a $5,000 bonus.

  Employee B is a vice president and is eligible to earn 40% of their annual salary. Employee B makes $100,000 per year and therefore is entitled to earn a $40,000 bonus.

- Commissions are typically associated with some type of sales, whether inside or outside sales. They may be tied to new or repeating business revenues. For instance:

  Employee A is an outside sales representative and can earn 2% of all new revenues. He/she generates $1,000,000 in new revenues and therefore is entitled to receive $20,000 in commissions.

- Commission payments vary and may be paid monthly, quarterly, or annually.

- Incentive programs vary and are typically associated with employees achieving specific goals that are often sales, performance or efficiency driven in nature. These goals are usually short term, although they can be measured annually.

Negotiating Salaries

*Next to interviewing, this has to be one of the most nerve-racking experiences that an individual will experience during the pre-employment phase. **Knowledge and confidence are the best tools that you can arm yourself with to successfully negotiate your salary.***

<u>Tips</u>

- Don't be afraid to discuss compensation.

- If you don't ask for what you want, you won't get it. For example, if an employer interviewing candidates for a job has an offer range of $40,000 to $50,000 per year, but the candidate asks for only $27,000, chances are the candidate will be offered less compensation less than may have been negotiated.

- Important Reality Check: Your previous earnings will play a significant role in determining what an employer will pay you. If you were earning $35,000 as a Marketing Assistant and you apply for a comparable Marketing Assistant role in another company, do not expect that they will be willing to pay you $60,000. The common exceptions to this rule applies to professional, typically licensed jobs, such as lawyers, accountants (CPAs), doctors, or engineers, first entering their specific field. Previous earnings may not have any impact.

- If there is no additional money for an employer to increase your base salary, you may be able to negotiate other terms such as an increased bonus potential (i.e., you currently receive a 10% annual bonus and you ask for a 15% annual bonus) or additional vacation time (i.e., you currently receive two weeks' vacation and you ask for three weeks' vacation). In other words, be creative.

- Although this will vary, common salary increase ranges may look like the following:

  a. New job at different company: 10% to 20% more than your last job. For instance, if you were making $50,000 then they may offer you $55,000 to $60,000.
  b. Promotions: 5% to 10%, unless there is a clearly defined graded compensation program. For instance, if you are a Sales Coordinator making $30,000, and you are promoted to a Sales Lead, you may see an increase of $3,000 to $33,000.

- For candidates and existing employees:

  a. See if you can obtain the salary range for the job you are currently in or are seeking.
  b. Have a history of your past 10 years' compensation written down as a guide for you to compare and reference in negotiation.
  c. A good rule of thumb, if moving into a comparable position, is to ask for 10 to 20 percent above what you made in your last job. If you made $30,000 in your prior role, for instance, ask for $36,000 in your new role.
  d. If you are moving into a role that is a promotion from your last role, and you made less than what
  e. is being offered in the new role, a good starting point is the base being offered for the new position or 20 percent above your last position; whichever is greater.
  f. If you are moving into a role that is a promotion from your last role and you made more than what is being

offered in the new role, a good starting point is 20 percent above your last position.

g. Remember that you can negotiate salaries lower from your initial request. Negotiating a salary higher than what you ask for is not likely to happen.

h. Everyone feels that they deserve more money. This doesn't mean that it is reasonable, logical, or practical. Remember, be realistic!

- For existing employees wanting raises:

a. Don't be afraid to ask for a raise, but... don't ask for one if it is not truly warranted and deserved.

b. Just because you performed your job doesn't warrant a raise. That is what you are supposed to do!

c. Just because you have been with an employer for some amount of time does not warrant a raise. This, unfortunately, is a misconception tied to the theory of annual performance reviews and raises.

d. Create a list of accomplishments between your last salary increase (or starting salary) and when you want to get a raise. This is how you will validate and sell your request.

e. If possible, try to demonstrate how you positively impacted the business by improving service, increasing sales, etc., above and beyond what is required. Keep in mind that the employer is in the business of making money, not losing money.

References

This is the moment where another person has the opportunity to validate or invalidate everything that you presented in your interview. **Your opportunities for employment most often hang in the balance when it comes to references.**

Tips

- Research what your previous employer's policy was related to providing references about former employees. Some allow for references to be given by employees, while some allow only for human resources to provide references. Others provide for only position and dates of employment to be provided. Many employers do not allow references at all.

- Be aware that although it is frowned upon, and often a violation of the law, to provide subjective (personal opinions and information not based upon fact) references about a former employee, it does happen. One day you are in the running for the job, the next you are out.

- Most employers will not provide you with information that they obtained during the course of reference checks.

- It is rare for an employer to accept personal references. Personal references usually include family and friends.

- If you have no previous work experience, provide a list of teachers and professors who can provide insight into your personality and educational practices.

- If you have work experience, it is highly recommended that you provide your most immediate supervisors or managers as references. These people will be most desired by the person conducting the background check, as they are usually the most knowledgeable of key information such as your performance, attitude, attendance and work ethic.

- Other good references to include are direct reports (people who reported to you), clients or customers (people to whom you provided services), and vendors who worked with you.

- Try to construct a list of references that can provide positive feedback about your experience.

- Make a list of at least 5 references, including their name, title, phone number, email address, and relationship to you (i.e., supervisor, direct report, peer, client, etc.). It is also a good idea to have the phone number of the Human Resources Department in the event the company policy prohibits references from being given out.

- Be sure to contact all individuals that you identify and give them a head's up that they may be contacted to provide a reference on your behalf. Give them some insight into the job and the company that you are interviewing for. Do not ask anyone to provide inaccurate or false information about you or your work performance. This will most surely backfire and result in problems down the road, including possible termination from your new job.

Background Checks

Beyond references, most employers want to have the comfort of knowing their employee's character is positive and in the company's best interest. This is most often achieved with a quick review of a person's criminal, civil and credit histories. ***In this electronic age, employers have access to just about anything about your life that they want.***

<u>Tips</u>

- Background checks may include any or all of the following:

  a. Criminal checks (local, county, state, federal, and/or military).
  b. Civil checks for lawsuits that do not involve criminal actions.
  c. Credit checks and your history of paying bills.
  d. Motor vehicle checks and your driving record.
  e. Terrorism database checks.
  f. Sexual offender database checks.
  g. Social security checks (typically used to confirm previous addresses).
  h. Professional licensing (i.e., lawyers, accountants, physicians, etc.)

- Criminal background checks may be solicited via a document requesting authorization or fingerprinting.

- Laws do govern the use of background checks in employment. In most situations, you will need to provide your authorization, in advance, for an employer to be able to run your background. This form should also provide you with a list of the types of checks the employer will be conducting.

- Many forms seeking your authorization to conduct background checks have an opportunity for you to check that you would like a copy of the report. It doesn't hurt to request your own copy to review for accuracy.

- States vary in the amount and types of information that may be sought. For instance, some states allow for arrest records to be provided, while others only allow only arrests resulting in convictions to be reported. Some limit how far back the checks can go (in California, for instance, 7 years in most situations) when a 3rd party is used to obtain the information. It is important that you check with your state's specific laws related to background checks to understand what will be provided.

- When you are asked to provide any information related to having been convicted of a crime (via application or verbally), do not omit this it. Omissions of this information, when discovered, will almost guarantee that you will lose the job. If this applies, you always want to have an opportunity, in advance, to discuss and explain the situation with the Human Resources department.

- *Reality check:* Although employers may state that convictions are not an absolute bar from employment, in most situations, it will likely work against you. This does not mean, though, that you shouldn't try. Keep in mind the old saying "nothing ventured, nothing gained."

- Credit checks may be used to determine the stability of an employee or the potential for theft when having access to money or financial information. Candidates with negative credit (i.e., excessive collections, bankruptcies, etc.) may be interpreted as unstable, and thus may be passed over for employment. If you know that this check is being conducted, I would always recommend that you discuss and explain the results, in advance, with the Human Resources department.

Pre-Employment Assessments

Skills can be taught but personality cannot. Employers utilizing pre-employment assessments are typically attempting to see if you will be a personality fit with the company. **No matter how competent or great you may be, not fitting into the employee profile that the employer is seeking may lead to you being passed over for the job.**

<u>Tips</u>

- Like it or not, pre-employment assessments are becoming more widely used.

- The assessments are typically used to examine cognition, basic skills (i.e., math, language, etc.), personality, fit, integrity, honesty and potential.

- Assessment results accepted in one company may not be accepted by another. It all depends upon what that employer is seeking.

- No matter what you do, answer the assessments honestly. Most assessments tend to have a "lie detector" built into them. Thus, they are able to identify inconsistencies and the likelihood that you may be trying to outsmart or manipulate the results.

- Some commonly used assessments include the DISC, Myers-Briggs, and 16PF. Some employer's also utilize assessments that are designed specifically for them.

- There's a strong likelihood that the person who is charged with making the hiring decisions, or providing feedback to the hiring manager related to the assessment results, is not qualified when it comes to interpreting and applying the assessment results. Most assessments require training and certification, but this is often not sought out by employers.

- Although pre-assessment tools should only be a small part of the decision making process (i.e., decisions should include a combination of the interview, experience, ability to meet the requirements of the job, education, assessments, etc.), it is not necessarily uncommon for an employer to consider the results of the assessment to be the most important or deciding factor when hiring.

Drug Testing

There really isn't too much to say here that isn't common sense. If non-prescription drugs are detected in your system, you can pretty much kiss the job goodbye. A large number of employer's are embracing the use of drug testing during their pre-employment and employment periods. Testing is quick and easy and will likely catch drugs in your system. **Bottom line...the best line of defense is not to engage drug use.**

Tips

- "Just say no". Although I know this sounds cheesy and does not always fit into the lifestyles of the general public, the reality is that a large number of employees require that you pass a drug test before you will be hired. Fail this test, and you will be looking for another job.

- The drug tests that are commonly used can detect quite a few of the most commonly used narcotics, prescription, and non-prescription drugs.

- Common drug tests include urinalysis, or obtaining saliva, hair, and/or sweat samples.

- The ability to detect drugs in your system varies by the drug used. The detection periods also vary by the type of test, whether urine, hair, blood or oral fluids. If you are worried that you may have drugs in your system and you have a drug test coming soon, I would encourage that you seek out medical references to determine the detection periods for the specific drugs.

- Drug testing facilities are familiar with the various tricks people may attempt to beat the test. Just because they aren't watching doesn't mean that they don't have built in mechanisms to detect deception.

Job Offers

Although the job offer may seem to be your endgame, it is just the beginning. That said, it is still an exciting moment, as this is the employer's way of letting you know that all your hard work has paid off in the form of an employment offer. **If you have reached this point in the process... CONGRATS!!!**

<u>Tips</u>

- Job offers may be verbal (spoken), written (on paper), or extended as an employment contract which is usually reserved for the most senior members of management.

- A verbal offer tends only to require that you verbally accept or refuse the job. This may be done in person or over the phone.

- A written offer tends to possess such information as job title, salary, benefits, vacation and sick leave, to whom you will report and start date. Other information may include special terms such as relocation packages, education reimbursement, sign-on bonuses and agreements related to your employment. Written offers usually require that you sign and return them by a specific date to acknowledge that you accept the terms of the offer.

- Employment contracts are usually very specific and reserved for senior management and executives. These have very specific terms related to that person's job and responsibilities. If you receive an employment contract, it is always recommended that you have a qualified employment or labor lawyer review it before you sign it.

- Other items that commonly accompany your offer may include Non-Disclosure Agreements, Non-Compete Agreements, Invention Assignments, and Arbitration Agreements.

- Some offers are made on a "contingency basis". This usually indicates that the offer is good only if you pass or meet certain additional terms, such as positive references, clean background check or passing a drug test.

- If you have questions about your offer, do not sign until you have asked them. Once you have signed, you have agreed to the terms, and the employer is not obligated to provide anything beyond the terms of the offer unless specifically outlined in the Employee Handbook. If there is something that you would like clarified or added to the offer, be certain to ask.

- If there is something in the agreement that does not meet your expectations, you can always request that your expectations be considered. For instance, the employer may offer you $50,000 per year, but you would like $60,000, or the employer offers two weeks' vacation leave per year and you would like three weeks per year.

Chapter 3: The Employment Phase

The New Hire Process

This is the process that usually occurs in the first few days of your employment in an effort to complete necessary paperwork, introduce you to the company, introduce you to the people, and get you prepared for what is to come. **Think of the new hire process as your introduction to your new job.**

Tips

- Not all employers have a structured or official new hire process. Some basically have you sit down and complete paperwork, while others may take you through a thorough introduction to the company, its people, philosophies, visions and beliefs.

- The new hire process may be as brief as an hour or take several days or weeks. Some companies refer to this process as "onboarding".

- The new hire process may involve only you or a group of others hired during the same period.

- Always be sure to bring pen and paper during your first couple weeks of employment. Keep track and take notes of the information that is provided to you. This will be to your benefit as you move forward.

- If you have questions about the workplace, policies, procedures, people, Employee Handbook, benefits, etc., be sure to ask during this period. When possible, make a list of questions in advance. You may have a tremendous amount of information coming your way, and you may be overwhelmed.

- Be sure to bring any and all paperwork, documents or other items requested. These will likely be important to completing the new hire process.

- Be sure to bring a notebook to take notes. You may meet a lot of people, here about important policies or procedures, need to remember phone numbers, or just want to remember other tips or information that you receive.

Employee Paperwork

Employee paperwork is one of those formalities that everyone will experience in employment. Sometimes it's painless and other times it's painful. **Be prepared to spend time reviewing and completing a battery of documents when your start your new job.**

Tips

- There are only two documents that are usually required to be completed during the course of employment. These are the W-4 and the I-9.

- The W-4 is the document that will impact how you are paid; specifically, the information that will dictate your state and federal tax deductions (state and federal; i.e., single, married).

- Human resources and management who are not tax professionals or licensed accountants are not allowed to provide guidance related to the W-4. There are instructions provided on the form. If you have questions, you should seek out the guidance from a tax or licensed accounting professional.

- For a current copy and instructions for completing the W-4, you can visit the Internal Revenue Service's website at www.irs.gov/pub/irs-pdf/fw4.pdf.

- The Form I-9 is the document that will be used to establish your ability to work for an employer in the United States.

    a. The Form I-9 acceptable documents list changes occasionally. For a current list of acceptable documents and instructions for completing the I-9, you can visit the United States Citizenship and Immigration Services website at http://www.uscis.gov/files/form/i-9.pdf.
    b. The Form I-9 has sections that must be completed by the employee (or interpreter) and the employer.

- You will be required to provide identifying documents within the first 72 hours of employment. Although not always adhered to, an employee is required to terminate your employment if you do not provide this information. Make sure that you have these documents readily available.

- You will be required to provide a single document from List A or one document from each of Lists B and C to satisfy the identifying documents requirement of the I-9.

- Employers cannot demand that you provide a document from all three lists, nor can they specify documents from those lists that you must provide (i.e., driver's license and social security card). You must only comply with the requirements set out on the form.

- Other documents commonly associated with the new hire processes include:

  a. *Personal Information Questionnaire:* This information is typically used to collect data for EEO reporting and to enter into the Human Resources Information or Payroll System.

  b. *Non-Compete and Non-Solicitation Policy:* These agreements vary by state. Some states allow them, while others do not. Check with an employment lawyer if you have questions about signing this document. If enforceable in your state, it usually provides that when you leave the company, you cannot go to work for a competitor for some defined period of time and that you cannot solicit employees from the company to leave to work with you at the new company.

  c. *Receipt of Employee Handbook:* This form is simply to provide proof that the employer provided you with a copy of the Employee Handbook. This can be a defense later in the employment relationship for the employer, especially if you are terminated for a violation of the policies outlined in the Handbook.

  d. *Non-Harassment/Sexual Harassment Policy:* This policy document provides an overview of policies and procedures related to harassment in the workplace. It is important that you read and understand this document.

  e. *Non-Discrimination Policy:* This is the company's policy related to defining discriminatory actions in the workplace and their approach to dealing with complaints of discrimination.

  f. *Arbitration Agreement:* These agreements vary by state. Some states allow for them and others do not. Check with an employment lawyer if you have questions about signing this document. Arbitration agreements are intended to move legal actions from courts to arbitration. Arbitration often reduces damages and actions that can be sought. It is important to note that the arbitration laws vary from state to state.

g. *Designation of Medical Professional:* This is a form primarily used for workers' compensation purposes. If you have a personal physician, it is strongly recommended that you designate them as soon as possible. If you do not, and you are injured on the job, you may be required to go to the company's doctor.

h. *Acknowledgment of Receipt of Company Property:* Pretty straight forward. This document reflects that you agree that you have received company property (i.e., uniforms, computers, keys, phones, etc.).

i. *Unemployment Benefits Notice:* Some states provide pamphlets or documents that are available for distribution to employees related to their rights and the process of obtaining unemployment benefits.

j. *Company Sponsored Benefits Enrollment Information:* These are the forms where you will sign up for company sponsored benefits. (i.e., medical, dental, 401K, etc.). Pay close attention to these documents and enrollment your periods.

The Employee Handbook

For those that are religious, please do not be offended by my next statement. Consider your Employee Handbook to be your "Bible" when it comes to employment. This is one of the single most important, and most often ignored, documents that you will receive. **The Employee Handbook is the company's guide to your success.**

<u>Tips</u>

- Read your Employee Handbook from cover to cover!!! Ignorance of company policies and practices is not a defense. Many questions that you have, or will have, will be located in the Handbook.

- If you don't understand something in the Handbook, ask your Human Resources representative or manager. Do not guess.

- Chances are you will find everything you need to know about payroll, benefits, vacation, holidays, attire, discipline and other common questions in the Employees Handbook.

- This is also a good place to learn about how the company views and handles topics like harassment, discrimination, drugs and alcohol, complaints, internet, email, phones, privacy and other topics that can negatively impact your job if you are not aware.

- Once you sign your Acknowledgment of Receipt of your Employee Handbook, you have admitted that you are familiar with the rules of the company. Some companies also require that you sign a document acknowledging that you have read and understand the Employee Handbook. Make no mistake that this document will go to your employee file and will be relied upon if you violate any policies. Read and understand the Handbook!

Payroll

Payroll is probably one of the top three topics for employees entering the workforce or a new job. **Although there are a few that will claim to be working because they enjoy it, the reality is that most people work to receive a paycheck.**

<u>Tips</u>

- Payroll practices vary from employer to employer.

- Paychecks are usually given to employees on a weekly, bi-weekly (every two weeks), semi-monthly (twice per month) or monthly (once per month) basis.

- Some employers pay through the workweek that you are paid, some pay a week in advance, and some pay a week behind. I strongly encourage that you ask about your company's practices on the first day. There is nothing worse than waiting for a paycheck then finding out it will either (a) be paid a week or two later or (b) be short a week due to paying a week behind.

- It is important to learn what your company practice is related to paydays falling on a holiday. Some pay prior to that day, while others pay after. Ask to be certain.

- Be prepared for the shock and reality of taxes and deductions being taken from your gross pay. Suppose you make $20 per hour and work 40 hours during a payroll period. Even though you have earned $800, chances are you will not see an $800, take home paycheck. The employer will withhold required taxes (i.e., federal and/ or state personal income taxes, social security taxes, etc.)

and any contributions you make for company sponsored benefits (i.e., $100 per paycheck for health insurance, $75 per paycheck for 401K deduction, etc.). Out of $800, you may only receive $500. You can inquire with your payroll administrator to get an idea of what your pay will be.

- If you receive a paycheck, and you believe it is not correct (i.e., not all hours worked are paid, vacation or holiday pay weren't paid, overtime pay wasn't paid, etc.), let your company's payroll know immediately so they can address the potential error.

- Garnishments may also be deducted from your paycheck. These are usually for child and spousal support, taxes, student loan defaults, and loan obligations. It is important to know a couple of things about garnishments:

  a. Payroll does not dictate or control garnishments. They are ordered by a Court and can only be eliminated by a Court. Payroll merely follows the directions of the order.
  b. Some states allow that an employee can be terminated from employment if they have multiple garnishments (usually other than child and spousal support).

- Find out what your company's payroll practices are as related to Holiday Pay; specifically, how you will be paid if you work on a company designated holiday. Some merely pay regular wages, while others may pay time and a half or even double time. When you are eligible to begin receiving pay for holidays that you do not work (some employers begin paying for these days at hire, others do not), influences your paycheck.

Employee Benefits

Employee benefits tend to be in the top three of priorities for employees entering the workforce or a new job. **Benefits are especially important as they refer to medical, dental and other desired advantages that will impact the lives of the employees and their families.**

<u>Tips</u>

- Companies are not always required to offer employees benefits. This does vary by federal, state and local laws. This arena will be going through many changes with the implementation of Obamacare.

- Benefits are a significant expense when it comes to businesses. Many employers pay anywhere from 50% to 90% of the costs of the medical benefit premiums, especially medical. These costs are usually derived from the experience of the employer, or their track record for costs of medical services paid on behalf of their employees.

- Due to the rising costs of medical insurance premiums, some employers only cover a percentage of the cost of the employee. This means that an employee will often be responsible for paying for a majority, or all, of dependents on the plan.

- The cost of employee contribution varies by employer. For instance, if a plan costs $1,000 per month, and the employer pays 80%, you will be responsible for paying $200 per month.

- Some employers will provide coverage for employees only, while others will allow for coverage of employees and their dependents.

- Some commonly offered company sponsored benefits include medical, dental, life, vision, supplemental, retirement, and legal plans.

- Here are some examples of common plans offered by employers:

    a. Medical HMO (Health Maintenance Organization)

        - Type of managed healthcare system.
        - Usually lower out of pocket cost for employee.
        - Tends to focus on preventive and wellness care.
        - Usually no lifetime, maximum payout.
        - Generally required to use specific physicians and facilities in the HMO network.
        - Non-HMO providers are not usually covered.
        - Typically required to select a PCP (Primary Care Physician).
        - Often requires referral to see specialists.
        - Typically requires a copay for services rendered.

    b. Medical PPO (Preferred Provider Organization)

        - Managed healthcare system
        - Uses a network of physicians and hospitals, though employees may use providers outside the network.
        - The cost for using out-of-network providers is typically more than those in the network.

- Payments are usually in the form of deductibles, co-insurance and co-pays.
- Co-insurance and co-payments may be a set rate or percentage of the total cost of care.
- For instance, an office visit may have a co-pay of $35 or co-insurance of 30% of the office visit costs (i.e., if the visit is $500, then you would pay $150).
- Typically, your out-of-pocket costs are limited.

c. DMO (Dental Maintenance Organization). This is basically the HMO of dental plans.

- Usually operates on a capitation plan, meaning that dentists get paid a set amount regardless how many times you visit them. The more you visit and more work they perform, the less they get paid.

d. PDO (Preferred Dental Organization). This is basically the PPO of dental plans.

- Includes a group of dentists that have agreed to set rates for specific treatments and processes.

e. Supplemental Insurance (i.e., AFLAC):

- Insurance that often pays participant cash benefits for specific events.
- Can assist with the costs of daily living, when you are sick or hurt.
- It is separate and independent of your other healthcare plans.

- Examples of supplemental insurance programs may include cancer, accidents, hospital indemnity, short term disability, and dental.
- AFLAC is a great example of supplemental insurance plans.

f. 401K Plans:

- A 401k refers to a retirement plan that is designed to provide an employee with a diversified portfolio of investments.
- Employees typically get to choose from a variety of investment options.
- Some employers provide matching funds to a certain amount, usually as a percentage, while others do not. For instance, the employer may match your contributions 100% on the first 5% of your contributions. If your employer offers matching funds, think of this as free money.
- Participation in 401k plans is usually optional although some employers will enroll their employees at hire. Employees being automatically enrolled usually have the choice to opt out.
- 401k plans may or may not be pre-taxed benefits.
- Don't touch your 401k savings unless you have no other choice. You may be taxed heavily.
- Some 401k plans allow for loans to be taken out against what has been saved. You will need to check with your plan administrator for specifics and qualifying reasons for these loans. Loans must be paid back.

g. Short and Long Term Disability Plans:

- Insurance for short and long term periods where an employee may be rendered disabled from working.
- Short term benefits typically last about 6 months.
- Benefits may start at your current rate of pay and reduce to a lower percentage of your salary after a specified period of time. For instance, during the first month of disability you receive 100% of your salary; during the third month you begin receiving only 80% of your salary. During the sixth month you may begin receiving only 60% of your salary.
- Long-term disability benefits begin when short-term disability benefits end. This benefit can be paid for years.
- Long-term disability plans may have an exclusionary period for pre-existing conditions. Once this period expires, the condition becomes covered under the plan.

h. Life Insurance (for self and dependents):

- Some employers offer employer paid benefits for employees. For instance, they may offer a fixed amount of all employees (e.g., $30,000) or 1, 2 or 3 times the employee's annual salary (e.g., employee A makes $50,000 per year and the employer offer 3 times their salary or $150,000).
- Your employer may offer the opportunity to obtain additional life insurance for yourself, your spouse or your dependents. The cost of additional insurance is usually paid entirely by the employee.

- The life insurance company may have a cap on the amount of life insurance benefits that you can obtain.

i. Employee Assistance Programs:

- Plans that provide an array of services and discounts on services to employees such as legal assistance, mental health and counseling and financial planning. EAPs also often operate as a referral service for employees to specialists in any or all of the above areas.
- These plans may be company, employee or a contributory combination of employee/employer paid.

j. Education Reimbursement Programs:

- This is a benefit that some employers provide to their employees in an effort to improve morale and business related skill sets.
- The amounts offered per year or program varies greatly, as well as the eligibility and payment options.
- Many of these programs have a clause built into them requiring an employee to remain with the company for a certain period of time after the reimbursement and with the provision that if they do not, they will be required to reimburse the employer for all benefits received for education.
- If your employer offers this benefit, take full advantage of it.

k. Employee Referral Rewards Programs:

- These benefits are usually established to encourage employees to refer other qualified candidates to the company for employment.
- This is a great way for employers to reduce the costs associated with recruiting. Rewards paid for referrals vary greatly from company to company.
- You will need to refer to your Employee Handbook or Human Resources Department for more information if employee referral rewards are offered by your company.

- For all benefits, pay close attention to eligibility requirements and benefits enrollment periods. Most benefits have a small window of opportunity to enroll or to modify each year. If you miss these deadlines, you will likely have to wait until the following year's open enrollment period.

Paid Time Off

The third topic that tends to be at the top of an employee's list is paid time off. **PTO includes such things as vacation, sick leave, personal time off and holidays.**

<u>Tips</u>

- An employer is not required to provide any paid time off for vacations, sick leave, holidays, personal time or otherwise. They are only required to pay you for the hours that you work. Keep in mind that this primarily applies to hourly, non-exempt, employees, as salaried personnel are typically required to work an undefined number of hours.

- Paid time off may include any or all of the following:

  a. Vacation
  b. Sick leave
  c. Personal days (i.e., birthday, anniversary, etc.).
  d. Paid time off (combination of vacation, sick, and personal leaves)
  e. Holidays
  f. Bereavement (for death of a family member)
  g. Sabbaticals

- Although not as common, some employers provide special paid leaves for events such as:

  a. Pregnancy/birth of a child/adoption of a child
  b. Marriage
  c. Care for a sick or injured family member

- Vacation, sick leave, personal days, and PTO may or may not be considered and treated as compensation. Thus, some or all of these may not be subject to "use-it-or-lose-it". Check with your state's regulations for more information.

- Read your Employee Handbook for specific information related to paid time off policies and practices. If your employer does not have a Handbook, ask your Human Resources Department or Manager.

Leaves of Absence

Most people, including many employers, usually do not have an idea of the various federal and state leaves of absence that are afforded to employees. **Many states actually have quite a few special Leaves of Absence that employees may be eligible for such as pregnancy, disability, witness duty, jury duty, domestic violence survivor or victims of crimes.**

<u>Tips</u>

- Your Human Resources Department will usually be the best source of information related to leaves of absence. Do not expect your manager to be aware.

- Your Employee Handbook may or may not have a list of leaves of absence and eligibility for those leaves.

- Some leaves of absence are paid while others are not.

- Some leaves of absence require continuation of benefits and seniority. Others do not.

- Some leaves are protected and required by law.

- Sometimes you will need to seek outside resources to learn if your state has a special leave for a specific situation that you may be experiencing.

- Some employers provide non-legally required leaves of absence for their employees. You will need to speak with your Human Resources Department for more information and eligibility requirements.

- If it is not required by law, an employer is not obligated to provide you with any special leaves of absence (those not dictated by law).

- Examples of common federal or state leaves of absence are for (varies by state) :

  a. Military leaves
  b. Jury and witness duty

c. Medical issues (to care for self or family member) including injury and sickness
d. Disability
e. Domestic violence and victims of crime
f. Pregnancy and maternity
g. Adoption

Disciplinary (Corrective) Actions

Disciplinary actions are probably the most dreaded, misunderstood, stressful and biggest anxiety creating topics that an employee may encounter during the course of their employment. **These actions refer to an arsenal of events such as warnings, demotions, probations, suspensions and terminations.**

Tips

- Discipline comes in many shapes…verbal warning, written warnings, probation, suspension, demotions, reduction in salary and termination.

- Your Employee Handbook is a great place to learn about what will land you in the disciplinary process. This is often found under the heading of "Prohibited Conduct".

- Attitude is everything! The wrong attitude, as perceived by your manager, may dictate your introduction to corrective actions. It is important to get this concept into your head. If your manager doesn't like your attitude, you are likely heading for a world of pain.

- Establishing violations of specific policies and performance issues are usually pretty easy to determine. This only constitutes a part of the events that result in corrective actions. It's the events involving attitude, and the concept of insubordination, that are usually a matter of interpretation. These will most likely be interpreted by your manager.

- If your company doesn't have a specified Progressive Discipline Policy (i.e., a specific order of corrective actions that must be taken in a specific order), they are usually able to engage any type of discipline they feel is necessary. This means that on offense one, termination may be in the cards.

- Just because someone was treated a certain way when they violated the same policy as you does not guarantee that you will be treated the similarly. Remember, business is not fair. Make no mistake that the employer will find all factors about the other employee's conduct that will distinguish their case from yours.

- Once you are on the bad side of a manager, chances are you are doomed, or at least destined, for a period of painful employment. The best advice is to make amends with that manager to the best of your ability.

- When you are presented with a written document outlining your violations and corrective action, you will likely be asked to sign the document. Many employees believe that if they don't sign it, that the document will be invalid or worthless. This is a myth. Your decision not to sign the document has no bearing on the action.

- If you disagree with the corrective action being taken against you, be sure to prepare a written response, including your supporting information, to accompany the documentation going into your personnel file.

- Most managers are uncomfortable when it comes to delivering corrective actions. Some will act tough and emotionless, while others will be passive.

- When you are receiving a corrective action, even termination, the worst thing you can do is blow up. Keep your cool and maintain your composure. If you don't, you can and will likely make things worse. Nothing is accomplished with yelling, screaming or threats.

- Chances are your Human Resources Department will be charged with giving you your corrective action. Keep in mind that the HR Department is most often merely the messenger. They are acting on behalf of your manager. Their knowledge is typically limited to the information that was provided to them.

- Don't expect a warning to clearly outline what the problems are. Often the warnings contain vague information such as "violated company policy".

- Don't expect for a warning to teach or provide you with guidance on how to correct problems. Managers tend to miss that if you didn't do it right the first time, maybe you don't understand how to do it.

- Common corrective action terms translated:

    a. *Insubordination*: This term is most often used when a manager can't objectively assign a violation of any company policy or procedure AND they either (a) don't like you, (b) don't like your attitude, or (c) both a & b. Bottom line...frustrating and usually lacking merit or substance.

b. *Not a fit*: This is another subjective term often used as a cop out when there is nothing of substance to establish that an employee should be terminated. This is usually code for "I don't like something about you and don't have a really good reason to terminate you, so I will terminate you by taking the easy way out."

c. *Performance*: This may or may not be subjective. If possible, have the individual providing the corrective action clarify what the performance issue was, whether or not the desired performance to accomplish or exhibit was provided to you, and what they are relying upon to support that there is a performance issue.

- Keep a copy of all emails and documents related to negative employment actions such as warnings, performance issues and discipline. These may be critical later, in the event you are subject to wrongful termination. If you don't keep these records, there is a strong likelihood they will be eliminated by the employer.

Corporate Structure

Although organizations vary in structure, there are some commonly recognized roles that are present. **As common as these roles may be, it is not uncommon for employees to be unaware of their existence or their functions.**

Tips

- The top group of managers in most organizations includes those who report directly into the President and CEO of the company. The titles of those direct reports vary by company and may include C-Suite to managers. These individuals most often are responsible for managing a major function or business group within the business.

- The top positions in the corporate structure are typically referred to as the "C-Suite". The following are the most common:

  a. *President and Chief Executive Officer (CEO):* This is top of the chain. Some organizations separate the roles into two, but often you will see them merged as one.
  b. *CFO (Chief Financial Officer):* This is one of the closest people to the President/CEO, as this person is responsible for the company finance and accounting.
  c. *COO (Chief Operating or Operations Officer):* This is usually the person responsible for managing the operations of the business.
  d. *CAO (Chief Administrative Officer):* Generally manages three or more support functions such as finance/accounting, human resources, IT, marketing, etc.
  e. *CTO (Chief Technology Officer) or CIO (Chief Information Officer):* This is the individual responsible for computer, network, hardware, software, phone systems and related functions and strategies.

- Other C-Suite positions that are not as commonly seen may include:

  a. CMO (Chief Marketing Officer)

    b.   CBO (Chief Business Officer)

    c.   CHRO (Chief Human Resources Officer) or CPO (Chief People Officer)

- Not all companies have an abundance of "C-Suite" positions. These organizations often have senior or executive teams that may include and/or all of the following:

    a.   SVP (Senior Vice President)/EVP (Executive Vice President).

    b.   VP (Vice President)

    c.   Senior Director/Director

- Other commonly observed management roles in a corporation may include *Lead, Supervisor* and/or *Manager*.

- There are other key corporate roles that may or may not have a manager-like title such as:

    a.   *General Counsel:* This is the individual who is the chief or head lawyer for the company.

    b.   *Controller:* This person is responsible for some or all aspects of accounting and finance. Sometimes, it may be in place of a CFO, and other times it may manage a specific facet of finance and accounting (i.e., reporting) for the CFO.

- Not all management positions are responsible for managing people. These positions are usually responsible for managing a specific product, customer or related item, such as an Account Executive, Account Manager, Sales Executive and Product Manager.

Corporate Departments

It always amazed me that employees can work for a company for 20 years and never have an idea of what their peers and other parts of their company do. **More shocking are employees sitting within 10 feet of each other who have no idea what the other person is responsible for.**

<u>Tips</u>

- It is important to have a basic understanding of what types of departments may exist in your company and what they do. Common departments within a company include:

    a. *Operations:* Typically responsible for conducting the revenues generating elements of the business. This may include corporate or field roles (i.e., restaurants, retail units, etc.) such as call centers, warehouses, distribution, facilities, and services.

    b. *Marketing:* Responsible for generating and managing such business needs as public relations, communications, advertising, marketing materials, tradeshows, etc.

    c. *Human Resources:* Responsible for such tasks as payroll, policies, benefits, recruiting, employee relations, and training.

    d. *Sales:* Responsible for selling the company's products or services. This may include inbound and outbound phone, field and travel based sales, or in person selling.

    e. *Finance and Accounting:* Responsible for such tasks as managing the company's money, budget preparation, banking, general ledger, taxes, accounts payable and receivable, and forecasting.

f. *Purchasing/Procurement:* Responsible for managing inventories, vendor contracts and relations, as well as purchasing equipment, supplies and services to ensure the company can conduct business.

g. *Legal:* Responsible for handling law based aspects of the company such as corporation formation, employment, securities, contracts, etc.

h. *Engineering:* Responsible for many aspects related to designing devices, machines, systems, processes, materials and related items for the business.

i. *Information Technology:* Responsible for managing all aspects of the infrastructure related to computers, software, hardware, systems, phones, networks, etc.

j. *Business Development:* Responsible for seeking out and developing new business, customers, and markets to increase revenues and company presence.

- Don't be afraid to talk to employees in other departments. Of course, don't do this when you are supposed to be working.

Dealing with Politics (Playing the Game)

Over the years, I have heard countless employees tell me how they refused to "play the game" and "get involved with the politics". Years later, it was not uncommon to see that they were no longer employed with the company or hadn't made much progress in relation to position and salary within the company. **Learn to play the game.**

Tips

- Your career will likely be tied to how well you fit into the company. Those who try to oppose or fight the politics tend to fall to the wayside or get passed over for advancement. Avoidance also leads to frustration and poor morale. PLAY THE GAME!!!

- Politics usually trumps ability and performance. This accounts for many company executives and managers being in their current roles. This, though, doesn't mean that you shouldn't perform. Engage the concept of "AND". Play the game "AND" while performing well.

- There is a difference between "brown-nosing" (kissing ass) and playing the game.

- Constantly opposing the company leadership and management will usually be seen as not being a "team player". This typically results in "political suicide" regardless of whether you are right or wrong.

- Sometimes is wiser to keep your mouth shut and your opinions to yourself. Believe it or not, even if you are right, your manager usually will not be excited about being wrong. You will not score points by proving your manager wrong.

- Subscribe to the old saying, "keep your friends close and your enemies closer." This is an excellent philosophy to embrace when it comes to corporate politics.

- Always be on the good side of the key decision makers in the company. It is wise to extend this philosophy to your immediate management as well.

Sexual Harassment

*This is unfortunately a hot topic and common event that occurs in the workplace. Sexual harassment can be extremely damaging to the person harassed and to the career of the harasser. **Best rule of thumb is to avoid it at all costs.***

<u>Tips</u>

- Sexual harassment is bad and certainly does not belong in the workplace!

- Sexual harassment can be engaged by any level of employee, from President to receptionist.

- It can involve non-employees such as customers, vendors, and independent contractors.

- It can be between employees who are the same gender (male/male and female/female) or opposite.

- Just because you don't think it is sexual harassment doesn't mean someone else won't. For example, imagine you blow a kiss at another employee, and they make a complaint against you for sexual harassment. Although inappropriate in the workplace, it may not be viewed as a serious offense to many people. Now, imagine that this employee was raped when they were 16 years old, and the attacker repeatedly blew kisses while raping them. Does this change your perspective?

- Sexual harassment is almost always a matter of perception of the person who feels harassed...not the harasser.

- Sexual harassment doesn't have to be done with the intent to harass.

- There are two basic types of sexual harassment in the workplace. These are quid pro quo and hostile work environment.

- Quid pro quo, or something for something, usually involves a manager and a subordinate (direct report) relationship. This basically means that the manager is a person who has the ability to influence the subordinate's employment, thus, having the ability to influence the hiring, firing, discipline, promotions, salary, etc., of the other employee.

- Hostile work environment pretty much refers to all other kinds of sexual harassment such as pictures, comments, gestures, blocking someone's movement, touching, massaging, sexual jokes, innuendos, repeatedly asking another employee on a date, and gender based stereotypes. In some states, simply staring at another employee can be considered sexual harassment.

- Even if you are not directing comments or gestures at someone, it can be considered harassment if they see or hear it.

- If you feel that you have been sexually harassed, report it to your Human Resources Department or Manager. It is always a good idea to review your company's complaint procedure related to sexual harassment. This should be found in your Employee Handbook.

- Most often, sexual harassment complaints come down to one person's word against another. Employees who harass with intent will usually ensure there are no witnesses and will cover their tracks with an alibi.

- Although retaliation for making a legitimate complaint of sexual harassment is usually a violation of labor laws, it does happen.

- Individuals can often be subject to personal lawsuit if they commit acts of sexual harassment. This may include criminal and civil action depending upon the specifics of the matter.

Discrimination

It still amazes me that discrimination, whether in the workplace or not, still has an active role in our society. **In the context of the workplace, whether a violation of law or not, it often plays a much larger role than most people think when it comes to decisions related to hiring, firing, promoting, management, and compensation.**

Tips

- Like harassment, discrimination is bad! The workplace should be free from harassing and discriminatory behaviors.

- Although much discrimination is unlawful, it does happen. Sometimes it is obvious, while other times it is not.

- There is lawful and unlawful harassment when it comes to the workplace. Not all types of harassment are illegal. This doesn't make it right, but it is what it is.

- In essence, discrimination means being treated differently than others due to being in a protected class (see below). In the workplace, this may include different treatment when it comes to such actions as hiring, promotions, wages, discipline, hours, benefits, hiring, lay-offs or otherwise.

- Protected classes tend to include:

  a. Race
  b. Ethnicity
  c. Religion
  d. Color
  e. National origin
  f. Disability status
  g. Veteran status
  h. Age (over 40)
  i. Genetic information
  j. Pregnancy
  k. Sexual orientation
  l. Sex/gender
  m. Marital status

- Protected classes may also vary from state to state, although some are federally protected under the Civil Rights Act of 1964, Equal Pay Act of 1963, Vietnam Era Veterans Readjustment Assistance Act of 1974 and related U.S. anti-discrimination laws.

- If you feel that you have been subject to unlawful harassment, you should always refer to your Employee Handbook or Human Resources Department for the appropriate steps to take. Be sure to act as quickly as possible.

Training

This has to be one of the most neglected areas in employment.
Inadequate training is one of the biggest contributors to poor
performance, low morale, high employee turnover and frustration.

<u>Tips</u>

- Don't assume that your employer will provide you with any, or adequate, training to perform your job. If you do receive training, listen closely and learn!

- Take the initiative to learn more about your role, company, business and industry. This may mean seeking external resources and education. Sometimes, employers provide reimbursement for work related training and education.

- If your company provides the option to gain new skills through company training, take advantage of it.

- If and when possible, cross train into other aspects of the business. The more that you can provide to the employer, the better your chances for continued employment and promotion.

- Even if you do not have a chance to use your newly acquired skills in your current role, they may come in handy for future roles and opportunities.

- If you are looking to move into a management role, learn about budgets, forecasting and managing a profit and loss (P&L) statement.

Dating in the Workplace

When it comes to dating in the workplace I always remember my dad's words of wisdom... "Don't dip your pen in the company ink."

<u>Tips</u>

- It's no secret that the average worker will spend 20 to 25% of their life between 18 and 68 years of age in the workplace. This said, it is not uncommon for relationships between coworkers to occur.

- Some companies have policies prohibiting dating in the workplace altogether. Check with your Employee Handbook or Human Resources Department before dating.

- Some companies only prohibit dating between management and their direct reports. This is usually due to the risk of sexual harassment claims (quid pro quo) due to the power a manager has over their subordinates.

- Most relationships in the workplace end in disaster. If a relationship goes bad, there is a strong likelihood that there will be tension, hurt feelings and gossip. This usually ends in one or both of the people resigning or being terminated.

- If you are a manager and you date a direct report (a subordinate), you are setting yourself up for career suicide whether or not the company prohibits the relationship. Even if the direct report is the initiator of the relationship, you will be at fault and YOUR career will be the one that suffers.

- If you think you can conceal a workplace relationship, you are wrong. Someone always finds out!

Workplace Injuries and Illnesses

Welcome to the world of workers' compensation. **This is the area of employment that provides employees with protection and coverage when they become ill from, or injured, in the course of employment.**

<u>Tips</u>

- Employees who are injured during the course of their work, or become ill due to a workplace event, may be eligible to receive workers' compensation benefits.

- Some states do not require workers' compensation coverage to be extended to business owners, independent contractors, unpaid volunteers or domestic employees in homes.

- Typically, these benefits are available, regardless of who is at fault.

- In most states, employers are required to carry workers' compensation insurance and are required to pay for the premiums. Some states, though, do not require workers' compensation insurance if they have a small number of employees (i.e., 5 or less).

- Workers' compensation benefits are usually provided in return for not being able to sue the employer in court for injury or illness.

- Examples of injuries that may result in the denial of workers' compensation benefits may include such events as:

  a. Self-inflicted injuries.
  b. Injuries related to conduct violating company policies.
  c. Injuries sustained during the course of committing a crime.

- Workplace injuries do not necessarily have to be at the worksite. Employees may be eligible if injured during the course of other business activities, such as business travel or running company errands.

- Some states allow employees to select their own doctor, if you request this before or at the time of injury. Other states allow for employees to be sent to doctors selected by the employer.

- Do note that workers' compensation doctors are paid by the workers' compensation insurance. Do not assume that they are your friend or on your side.

- If you are injured while working, or become ill due to your workplace, contact your manager and/or Human Resources Department as soon as possible.

- Expect that a thorough investigation of your injury, including videos, witness statements, previous history of injuries, other activities that may have caused the injury, etc. will occur. There is a high frequency of workers' compensation fraud which has prompted the need for employers and insurance companies to conduct adequate due diligence to ensure that they are not being scammed.

- If you commit workers' compensation fraud, you can go to prison, pay stiff fees and court costs and have to repay all monies paid to you through benefits! Furthermore, you are likely going to be out of a job. If you are considering fraud, I would strongly discourage it.

- The following is a list of items that may flag a workers' compensation claim as being fraudulent:

  a. Not reporting the injury immediately.
  b. Financial hardship.
  c. The injury occurs on a Monday.
  d. Lack of witnesses.
  e. The story of how the injury occurred is inconsistent or not logical.
  f. The injury occurs with a disgruntled employee or one who has recently been disciplined.
  g. The employee does not show up to scheduled medical appointments.

Disabilities/Disabling Conditions

Disabilities come in many forms, shapes and sizes. Furthermore, they are more common in the workplace than most people realize. This is an often misunderstood area in employment, and it is important that employees and employers have a basic understanding of how they apply to the workplace. **This knowledge assists with ensuring that workplaces are not only void of discriminatory behaviors towards individuals with disabilities, but that the environments are conducive to accommodating all employees, regardless of disabling conditions that may exist.**

<u>Tips</u>

- Some disabilities are easy to identify, as they are able to be viewed, while others may not be as easy to see or recognize in the workplace.

- Some examples of potential disabilities may include:

  a. Depression
  b. Anxiety
  c. Blindness
  d. Epilepsy
  e. Paralysis
  f. Obsessive Compulsive Disorder
  g. Bi-Polar Disorder
  h. Diabetes
  i. Post-Traumatic Stress Disorder
  j. ADHD/ADD
  k. Sleeping Disorders

- Although definitions may vary from state to state, a disabling condition tends to refer to a circumstance that substantially limits a major life activity.

- A good interpretation of "substantially limiting" is that it refers to restrictions on how someone performs a major life activity as a result of an impairment or disabling condition making it difficult to perform that activity.

- Some examples of major life activities includes:

  a. Breathing
  b. Walking
  c. Sleeping

    d.   Thinking
    e.   Concentrating
    f.   Hearing
    g.   Learning

- The Americans with Disabilities Act (ADA) provides protection to employees who are treated as, or regarded as, having a disability or disabling condition. This protection also extends to individuals with a history of a disability.

- Under the ADA, employers with 15 or more employees cannot discriminate against qualified individuals with disabilities.

- Some states have additional, and/or broader classes of disabling conditions and criteria to determine if a qualified, disabling condition exists.

- You do not have to disclose your disability when you apply for a job (i.e., application, interview, etc.). This includes accommodations you may require when employed. You may, though, be asked on an application, or during the interview, if you can perform the functions of your job with or without reasonable accommodation.

- There are some potential exceptions where employers can inquire about potential disabling conditions. These must be after you are hired AND job related, and be consistent with business necessity. These requests, though, are limited in what can be asked. The following are some potential events that may trigger requesting this information.

    a.   If there is evidence that you are unable to perform the functions of your job.

b. If there is evidence that there may be a threat to the health or safety of yourself or others.

c. An injury on the job.

- Reasonable accommodations for individuals with qualifying disabilities may include such actions as modified work schedules, modifications of the work station or environment, job restructuring, time off to attend therapy or medical procedures, job coaching, special equipment or devices and transfers to other roles for which the individual may be qualified.

- Employers are only required to provide reasonable accommodations for disabled employees when they are known. In some circumstances, this knowledge may be implied. A good recommendation for an employee who is disabled is to notify the employer. I would encourage discussing with the Human Resources Department if possible.

- You may be required by your employer to provide a note from your doctor. This note usually needs to provide the doctors diagnosis that you have a disabling condition and instructions that you require accommodation. You do not have to provide your entire health or medical history.

- You will need to fully participate in the in the reasonable accommodation process. If you do not, there is a chance that you could lose your federal, and/or state rights.

- Although making the employer aware is a good idea, unfortunately you must be prepared for any of the following:

    a.   Discrimination.
    b.   Loss of privacy.
    c.   Stigmas.

- Disabilities discrimination is a reality! Although employers and managers will not admit it, individuals with disabling conditions are often seen as high maintenance and liabilities. This is extra time and commitment that they feel is not fair to their business operations.

- Disabilities discrimination may come in the form of such employment actions as not being hired, promoted, given additional duties, compensation increases, etc. Another less obvious method that employers may engage to discriminate includes submitting poor performance reviews against the disabled person in an attempt to validate the employer's position.

- If you need additional information about disabilities protection or believe that your rights have been violated based upon your disabling condition, please visit or contact the United State Equal Employment Opportunity Commission at www.eeoc.gov or (800) 669-4000.

Miscellaneous Things to Know

It would be practically impossible to catch everything about the workplace in a single book. **That said, here are some other practices and concepts that may be good to know.**

<u>Tips</u>

Hourly (non-exempt) vs. Salaried (exempt) Employees

- There are two terms that you should really know when it comes to being paid:

  a. Non-exempt: Basically, this means that you are paid by the hour and are entitled to receive overtime pay (and double-time pay where applicable) for overtime hours worked. Overtime calculations vary from state to state

  b. Exempt: This is often referred to as "salaried" and means that you are not entitled to receive overtime pay for excess hours worked.

- Employers are aware of the perceived importance employees equate with being "salaried" versus "hourly".

- Don't be fooled into thinking that a "salary" is a great thing. All that this means is that you will likely not receive overtime pay for the 10 to 25 hours you work additionally per week.

- A large number of "salaried" employees are actually misclassified, and are eligible, to receive overtime pay. Classifying employees as "salaried" is often just a way for employers to overwork employees without paying them their entitled compensation. This has been a major topic in employment litigation for the last decade.

- The requirements for being classified as an exempt employee, or a person not being entitled to receive pay for overtime hours worked, vary from state to state. Some states have very strict requirements for being classified as exempt, while others rely on the federal government's requirements.

- A significant factor that influences being an exempt employee is that the employee does not do tasks that are commonly performed by hourly employees or subordinates.

  For instance, in a restaurant, an exempt manager may not be allowed to run the cash register, clean off tables or cook food, as this may disqualify them as being exempt, and thus make them entitled to receive overtime pay. Again, exempt status requirements vary from state to state.

- Non-exempt employees are usually subject to specific rules and regulations related to meal periods and rest periods or breaks.

Performance Reviews

- Chances are that your manager has never been taught how to review someone's performance. This process is usually referred to as Performance Management or a Performance Review.

- Chances are your manager does not want to have to review your performance. This is usually because of the amount of time it takes to appropriately review performance, the manager doesn't understand how to conduct the review, and they are uncomfortable reviewing a subordinate's performance or some combination of the above.

- Positive performance reviews do not guarantee that you will receive a salary increase.

- Chances are that once you have received your performance review, you will never see it again; unless, of course, you're being fired.

- Performance reviews are often a reflection of your manager's current opinion of you (do they like you or not when they are reviewing you) and less about your actual performance over the course of the previous year.

- Always ask for a copy of your review. Keep it in a file at home. You never know when you may need to refer to it.

Advancement and Growth

- Don't expect the company to recognize you for your performance and dedication. If you want to advance and grow, you will likely have to ask for it.

- Get used to people making more money than you when they join the company after you. The more time that passes, the more likely that the new employees will receive a higher starting wage.

- If you want to earn more money, staying in one company for 20 years is usually not the answer. Employees staying in one company for extended tenures of 10 or more years often only see 0 to 5% annual increases in their pay, whereas employees moving to new companies every 3 to 5 years tend to experience 10 to 20% increases with each move, with this in addition to the annual increases they may receive at their current company.

- College degrees, advanced and professional degrees, and certifications can assist you with attaining bigger positions, more responsibility, bigger titles and more money. Although not a guarantee, I would strongly encourage any or all of the above.

Termination of Employment

Termination of the employment relationship means that you no longer work for that employer. **Termination comes in several forms including resignation, lay-off, termination and retirement (and death, but we will not need to discuss this way out).**

<u>Tips</u>

- This is the end of the line. It may be due to your choice or not. It may include resigning or retiring. It may include termination or lay-off.

- Termination At-Will: In essence, this means that an employee or employer may terminate the employment relationship, with or without cause, and with or without notice. In other words, they can terminate you without a reason and without informing you of their intent.

- The two most common exceptions to at-will termination include:

  a. *Terminations contrary to public policy:* These are often the basis for wrongful termination lawsuits. In other words, you were terminated because you engaged a legally protected activity and were terminated based on a discriminatory action, etc.
  b. *An employment contract:* Written contracts tend to outline the terms and obligations related to termination. Implied and verbal contracts are usually difficult to prove. If you believe that you have an implied or verbal contract, and you are terminated, you should consult a qualified employment lawyer.

- Termination for Cause: This usually refers to a termination that is based upon an employee violating company policies and procedures or poor performance. Although not a guarantee, there are often accompanying warnings, verbal or written, related to previous or current violations. It is always encouraged that you refer to your Employee Handbook for a list of actions that will land you in this arena...usually under the heading of "Prohibited Conduct".

- Lay-offs are certainly a reality in our economy. This termination refers to being released from service due to economic problems, restructuring, redundancy of roles or no longer being necessary to the business's bottom line.

- Final paychecks: States vary by their final paycheck practices. Some require that final paychecks are provided on the last day of work while other states provide that paychecks can be delivered to you on the company's next, usual payday. Check with your state for specific laws related to final paychecks.

- If you are an employee who receives commissions, you will need to seek out additional information from your state to find rules pertaining to payment of pending commissions. Also, be sure to check with your company's policies regarding commissions due during and after employment.

- Unreturned property and outstanding company debts: Some states provide that an employer can deduct from an employee's final paycheck for unreturned company property or debt that an employee may owe to the company. On the other hand, some states do not allow this, thus forcing employers to seek out their losses in court. Again, you will need to check with your state's specific laws about deductions from your final check.

- If possible, obtain a copy of your entire employee file on your final day of work. Some states have specific laws related to what the employer must provide when requested. For instance, some only require the employer to provide copies of documents that you signed.

- Don't make a scene or cause trouble on your last day, even if you were fired and disagree with the decision. This will not be in your favor.

- Find out what the company policy is related to references. It is important to have an idea of what information will be provided to future employers conducting background and reference checks. A common practice of companies is to only provide your job title dates of employment.

- See if the company has an outsourcing program to assist you with the transition. Take any assistance you can get to regain employment.

- Some companies provide a severance package when they release employees via lay-offs and terminations. This usually includes the continuation of pay, and/or benefits for a specified number of weeks or months. This is not required by law. If you do receive the offer for severance, you will likely be required to sign a release of liability, thus getting the pay for waiving your rights to sue the employer in the future.

Chapter 4: The Post-Employment Phase

Surviving Unemployment

Being out of work can be a highly stressful event for most people. The lack of income alone can be catastrophic, often resulting in the loss of homes and property as well as serious strains on personal and family relationships. **Being prepared to navigate through the unemployment period is critical!**

<u>Tips</u>

- Unemployment is stressful, but not the end of the world.

- Once you become unemployed, it is imperative that the mourning period is short and that you become focused on becoming employed again as quickly as possible. Sitting around feeling sorry for yourself will not do you any good.

- If you are married or in a relationship, sit down with your partner and discuss strategies to get through unemployment. You need to have a collective front to successfully cope with this period. Make a list of all of your resources, financial obligations and available money.

- Be prepared to significantly alter your spending habits. Conservation of money is vital. If you don't have to spend it…DON'T!

- If you are eligible to receive unemployment benefits, file as soon as possible. Many states have waiting periods before you will receive your benefits.

- Sit down and prepare an updated resume immediately. You will need hard copies as well as an electronic copy to submit to potential employers online.

- File with as many local temporary agencies as possible. This will take a few days, but this increases your opportunities for temporary and possibly direct hire employment. Some agencies also provide benefits to their temporary employees after meeting certain requirements.

- Seek out local, regional and national recruiters. Register and provide them with a copy of your resume.

- Visit local workforce assistance centers. States, churches and some non-profit organizations provide these services free of charge.

- Refer to Chapter 2 for pre-employment guidance and resources.

What Happens to Your Health Coverage (An introduction to COBRA)

Termination of employment is often magnified due to the loss of employee benefits, especially medical benefits when an employee has children, preexisting conditions or current health problems. ***It is important to understand how the continuation of benefits works to ensure that you and your dependents are protected.***

Tips

- If you were enrolled in company sponsored medical benefits, you will most likely receive a notice of COBRA within 14 days of your termination.

- COBRA is short for Consolidated Omnibus Budget Reconciliation Act.

- COBRA usually applies to private-sector companies with at least 20 employees.

- COBRA was designed to provide former employees, dependents (spouse, children, and former spouse) and retirees the ability to enroll in temporary continuation of their health coverage at group rates when coverage is lost due to certain specific events.

- For employees, qualifying events for COBRA include such events as:

    a. Termination of employment (termination for misconduct may be a disqualifying event).
    b. Reduction in the number of hours the employee works.

- For spouses, qualifying events for COBRA include such events as:

    a. Divorce.
    b. Legal separation.
    c. Termination of employment (termination for misconduct may be a disqualifying event).

d.   Reduction in the number of hours the employee works.

e.   The employee becomes eligible for Medicare.

f.   Death of the employee.

- For children, qualifying events for **COBRA** include such events as:

  a.   Child is no longer covered as a dependent child.

  b.   Divorce or legal separation.

  c.   Termination of employment (termination for misconduct may be a disqualifying event).

  d.   Reduction in the number of hours the employee works.

  e.   The employee becomes eligible for Medicare.

  f.   Death of the employee.

- You have 60 days to decide whether or not you will elect **COBRA**, and 45 days to pay the initial premium after electing the coverage.

- Employers or plan administrators can charge up to 102% of the cost of the premium. The 2% is for administrative costs.

- You will likely be shocked when you see the costs of continuing your benefits at the full premium dollar amount. Keep in mind that many employers pay a significant percentage of the costs of benefits. For example, you may have been paying $200 per month for medical coverage when employed, but the employer was paying $800 (total premium of $1,000). Under **COBRA** you will have the entire premium, and possibly an extra 2% on top.

- COBRA benefits usually last a maximum of 18 months. There are exceptions that allow for extensions up to 36 months for certain qualifying events.

- For more information about COBRA benefits, you can visit the Department of Labor's website at www.dol.gov.

- If you opt out of COBRA, you can find alternatives such as personal health coverage. Many can be researched online, through local insurance brokers or state sponsored healthcare programs and plans.

- If you choose personal healthcare coverage, be aware that there are factors that may influence your ability to secure a cost effective plan (i.e., preexisting conditions, breaks in healthcare coverage, etc.).

Unemployment Benefits

Unemployment benefits are intended to assist unemployed or underemployed individuals with some financial assistance during these periods. These benefits are not guaranteed and are subject to state regulations. **Unemployment benefits are limited in duration, thus increasing your need to return to work as soon as possible.**

Tips

- These benefits are established to provide unemployed individuals, and employees with reduced work hours, temporary financial assistance.

- States administer their own unemployment benefits.

- There are criteria that must be met to qualify for unemployment benefits. Just because you are unemployed does not mean that you will be eligible to receive unemployment benefits.

- The amount of the benefits and period you will be paid benefits varies from state to state.

- Minimum eligibility for many states requires that an employee has worked for the previous four to five calendar quarters (12 to 15 months) prior to filing.

- Demonstrating that your unemployment is due factors other than your own choice or fault (i.e., resignation) is often another minimum criterion that must be met for benefits eligibility.

- Some states may deny unemployment benefits for terminations that are considered to be extremely bad (i.e., violence, sexual harassment, etc.) or directly in violation of clearly defined company policies (i.e., excessive absences, drugs and alcohol on company premises, etc.).

- In order to be eligible for these benefits, you must contact your state unemployment benefits agency. Claims for benefits may be conducted over the phone, online or in person.

- It is recommended that you file for unemployment benefits in the state that you actually worked.

- When you file, be prepared to provide information such as:

a. Dates of employment, including last day worked.
b. Reason that you are no longer employed.
c. Your compensation (salary or hourly wage).
d. Name and address of your former employer.

- It may take a couple weeks to process your initial claim. Be sure to file as soon as possible to begin receiving your benefits.

- Follow any and all direction provided by your state's unemployment benefits agency. They may require that you enroll or participate in training or related programs.

- Some employers will attempt to deny your claim, whether or not you are eligible to receive the unemployment benefits. If you are denied the initial claim, don't fret.

- If you are denied unemployment benefits, you will have the right to appeal the decision. The state's unemployment benefits agency will provide you with the appropriate process to appeal. Read these procedures closely and be sure to file your appeal within the given response period. Failure to follow the instructions may lead to denial of all unemployment benefits.

- Some states provide extended unemployment benefits during periods of high unemployment.

- Unemployment benefits are subject to federal taxes and must be reported on your federal income tax return.

Wrongful Termination

Unfortunately, wrongful termination is a real and common practice in the business world. **Although there are numerous laws to protect employees, employers know that they usually have more resources, money and time to battle out a matter in court.**

Tips

- Just because you don't agree with the termination doesn't make it wrongful termination.

- Wrongful termination tends to refer to being terminated based upon a protected class or activity. Examples of situations that may warrant wrongful termination may include termination, demotion, change in hours or other related negative employment action based upon:

  a. Age (if over 40)
  b. Pregnancy
  c. Making a valid complaint of sexual harassment or discrimination
  d. Being injured on the job
  e. Participating in an investigation or hearing related to harassment or discrimination
  f. Protected military, family medical (FMLA), disability or related leaves

- A significant number of managers do not properly prepare written warnings and termination documents. Those who do are usually not skilled at drafting them. This can be a potential advantage in a wrongful termination lawsuit.

- If you file a lawsuit for wrongful termination, do not be surprised to see documents that didn't exist during your employment or hear comments and statements that are not true. Employers do not tend to like to have to pay out money in litigation.

- If you think that all of your colleagues who were aware of your situation are going to testify on your behalf, think again. Even if they want to, most will be scared to lose their job for doing so.

- Don't ever think that a wrongful termination lawsuit is a slam dunk. There are always two sides, and most parties will do their best to defend their position.

- Employers usually have the resources, time, money and insurance to battle out a wrongful termination lawsuit. This unfortunately is not the same for most employees... which the employers know.

- If you believe that you have been wrongfully terminated, seek out a qualified employment lawyer as soon as possible to discuss your situation. Most employment actions have a statute of limitations. This means that you only have a certain amount of time to file a lawsuit.

- Many employment matters can be tried in a state or federal administrative employment agency such as Labor Boards, Equal Employment Opportunity Commission, Department of Fair and Equal Housing, Workforce Commission, etc. The advantage of some of these agencies is that they will conduct the investigations for the person making the complaint if they feel that the matter may be substantiated. This is often a good route for former employees who cannot afford legal counsel. (Refer to the Resources Section of the book for specific state agencies).

- Keep in mind that if you pursue litigation, the process is often lengthy and emotionally, psychologically and physically exhausting. Furthermore, it can lead to being blacklisted in small industries where news travels fast. This is not intended to deter you from taking the appropriate action, but to make you aware of the realities of litigation.

Chapter 5: Resources

Federal Labor and Employment Agencies

The United States Department of Labor (DOL) is responsible for administering Federal labor laws related to safe and healthy working conditions, minimum hourly wages, overtime pay, unemployment insurance, freedom from discrimination in the workplace and other forms of income support. This is done with the intent to ensure the welfare of people seeking employment, people currently earning a living and retirees.

<u>DOL Agencies</u>

- Administrative Review Board (ARB).
- Benefits Review Board (BRB).
- Bureau of International Labor Affairs (ILAB).
- Bureau of Labor Statistics (BLS).
- Center for Faith-Based & Community Initiatives (CFBCI).
- Employee Benefits Security Administration (EBSA).
- Employees' Compensation Appeals Board (ECAB).
- Employment and Training Administration (ETA).
- Mine Safety and Health Administration (MSHA).
- Occupational Safety and Health Administration (OSHA).
- Office of Administrative Law Judges (OALJ).
- Office of the 21st Century Workforce (21CW).
- Office of the Assistant Secretary for Administration and Management (OASAM).
- Office of the Assistant Secretary for Policy (OASP).
- Office of the Chief Financial Officer (OCFO).
- Office of the Chief Information Officer (OCIO).
- Office of the Inspector General (OIG).
- Office of Disability Employment Policy (ODEP).
- Office of Federal Contract Compliance Programs (OFCCP).

- Office of Labor-Management Standards (OLMS).
- Office of Workers' Compensation Programs (OWCP).
- Office of the Ombudsman for the Energy Employees Occupational Illness Compensation Program.
- Office of Small Business Programs (OSBP).
- Office of the Solicitor (SOL).
- Veterans' Employment and Training Service (VETS).
- Wage and Hour Division (WHD).
- Women's Bureau (WB).

DOL Contact Information

- Website: http://www.dol.gov/
- Phone Number: 1-866-4-USA-DOL
- TTY Number: 1-877-889-5627
- Mailing Address: U.S. Department of Labor 200 Constitution Ave., NW
- Washington, DC 20210

The Equal Employment Opportunity Commission (EEOC) enforces discrimination against job applicants and employees based upon color, race, national origin, religion, age (40 years old and over), sex (gender; also includes pregnancy), disabilities and/or genetic information. It also enforces discrimination against those who have made a complaint about discrimination, have filed a discrimination charge or who have participated in an employment discrimination investigation or legal action. Labor unions, employment agencies and employers with 15 employees or more are usually covered by the EEOC. You will need to confirm with qualified legal employment counsel, or the EEOC, if you have specific questions related to your situation.

<u>EEOC Contact Information</u>

- Website: http://www.eeoc.gov/
- Phone Number: 1-800-669-4000
- TTY Number: 1-800-669-6820
- Email: info@eeoc.gov
- *EEOC Field Office Locations Website:*
- http://www.eeoc.gov/field/index.cfm
- *EEOC Headquarters Contact:* U.S. Equal Employment Opportunity Commission131 M Street, NE Washington, DC 20507 Phone: (202) 663-4900,
- TTY: (202) 663-4494

State Employment and Labor Agencies

The following list provides the names of agencies, by state, that are charged with some facet of the administration of labor and employment laws and practices. These may include such areas as wage and hour, discrimination, retaliation, workers compensation, harassment, wrongful termination, unemployment, and disabilities.. Please note that each state may have additional agencies or divisions responsible for administration.

1. Alabama: Department of Industrial Relations.
2. Alaska: Department of Labor and Workforce Development.
3. Arkansas: Employment Security Department.
4. Arizona: Department of Economic Security.
5. California: Department of Fair and Equal Housing, Department of Industrial Relations, and Employment Development Department.
6. Colorado: Department of Labor and Employment.
7. Connecticut: Department of Labor.
8. Delaware: Department of Labor.

9. District of Columbia: Department of Employment Services.
10. Florida: Agency for Workforce Innovation.
11. Georgia: Department of Labor.
12. Hawaii: Department of Labor and Industrial Relations.
13. Idaho: Department of Commerce & Labor.
14. Illinois: Department of Employment Security and Office of Workforce Development.
15. Indiana: Department of Workforce Development.
16. Iowa: Office of Workforce Development.
17. Kansas: Department of Labor.
18. Kentucky: Office of Employment and Training.
19. Louisiana: Department of Labor.
20. Maine: Department of Labor.
21. Maryland: Division of Workforce Development.
22. Massachusetts: Division of Unemployment Assistance and Division of Career Services.
23. Michigan: Unemployment Insurance Agency, Workers' Compensation Agency, Division of Wage & Hour, and Department of Career Development.
24. Minnesota: Department of Employment and Economic Development, Unemployment Insurance and Local
25. Work Force Centers.
26. Mississippi: Department of Employment Security.
27. Missouri: Division of Employment Security.
28. Montana: Department of Labor & Industry.
29. Nebraska: Office of Workforce Development.
30. Nevada: Department of Employment, Training & Rehabilitation.
31. New Hampshire: Office of Employment Security.
32. New Jersey: Department of Labor and Workforce Development.
33. New Mexico: Department of Labor.
34. New York: Department of Labor.

35. North Carolina: Employment Security Commission.
36. North Dakota: Job Service North Dakota.
37. Ohio: Working & Employment portal.
38. Oklahoma: Employment Security Commission.
39. Oregon: Employment Department.
40. Pennsylvania: Department of Labor and Industry.
41. Rhode Island: Department of Labor and Training.
42. South Carolina: Employment Security Commission.
43. South Dakota: Department of Labor.
44. Tennessee: Department of Labor and Workforce Development.
45. Texas: Workforce Commission.
46. Utah: Department of Workforce Services.
47. Vermont: Employment Portal.
48. Virginia: Employment Commission.
49. West Virginia: Bureau of Employment Programs.
50. Washington: Employment Security Department.
51. Wisconsin Department of Workforce Development
52. Wyoming: Office of Workforce Security.

Family and Medical Leave Act (FMLA)

The Family and Medical Leave Act (FMLA) is a federal law that requires covered employers to provide an eligible employee up to a total of twelve work weeks of unpaid leave during any twelve month period and for any one or more of the following reasons:

- Birth and care of the newborn child of the employee.

- Placement with the employee of a son or daughter for adoption or foster care.

- Care for an immediate family member (spouse, child, or parent) with a serious health condition.

- Take medical leave when the employee is unable to work due to a serious health condition.

- Qualifying exigency arising out of the fact that the employee's spouse, son, daughter, or parent is a covered military member on "covered active duty".

- To care for a covered service member with a serious injury or illness if the eligible employee is the service member's spouse, son, daughter, parent or next of kin (military caregiver leave). The employee may be entitled to up to 26 work weeks of leave during a single 12 month period of time for this qualifying event.

Although it is always recommended that you seek qualified employment counsel for clarification of laws, the following is an overview of some key points of FMLA.

Eligibility

- An "eligible" employee is an employee who has been employed by the employer for at least twelve months and worked at least 1,250 hours.

- The twelve months do not need to be consecutive.

- An "eligible" employer refers to an employer who employs 50 or more individuals within 75 miles of the worksite.

Additional General Tips

- FMLA can be taken intermittently, thus providing the employee the ability to work on a less than full-time schedule

- Employees are entitled to have their benefits maintained during the FMLA leave, but they must continue to pay their portion during the leave, unless otherwise provided for by the employer.

- Employees also have the right to return to the same or equivalent position, pay and benefits at the conclusion of their leave. Although uncommon, some exceptions do apply to this rule.

- If an employee and their spouse both work for the same employer, both may not be entitled to each take twelve weeks off (each) for the birth of a child, when adopting a child or to care for a parent with a serious health condition, unless otherwise provided for by the employer.

- The employee is not responsible for designating FMLA leave. This is the employer's responsibility. That said, it is the employee's responsibility to provide a 30 days advance notice for foreseeable events. The employer can also ask the employee to provide certification from a medical provider testifying to the need for the requested leave. Additionally, once the leave is completed, the employer may request and require that the employee provide a certification of fitness to return to work if the leave was due to the employee's own health issues.

For more and specific information related to the FMLA, please visit the United States Department of Labor's website at www.dol. gov.

Americans with Disabilities Act Amendments Act of 2008

September 25, 2008, amendments to the Americans with Disabilities Act (ADA) were signed into law. These amendments were intended to clarify and reiterate who is covered by the law's civil rights protections. These amendments went into effect January 1, 2009.

Some key measures of the 2008 amendments include:

- Revises the definition of "disability" to more broadly encompass impairments that substantially limit a major life activity.

- States that mitigating measures, including assistive devices, auxiliary aids, accommodations, medical therapies and supplies (other than eyeglasses and contact lenses) have no bearing in determining whether a disability qualifies under the law.

- Clarifies coverage of impairments that are episodic, or in remission that substantially limit a major life activity when active, such as epilepsy or post-traumatic stress disorder.

- Restricts an employer's use of qualification standards based upon uncorrected vision standards.

- Defines "major life activities" as including, but not limited to, caring for oneself, performing manual tasks, seeing, hearing, eating, sleeping, walking, standing, lifting, bending, speaking, breathing, learning, reading, concentrating, thinking, communicating and working.

- Defines "major bodily functions" as including, but not limited to, functions of the immune system, normal cell growth, digestive, bowel, bladder, neurological, brain, respiratory, circulatory, endocrine and reproductive functions.

For more information related to the Americans with Disabilities Act Amendments Act of 2008, please visit the United States Department of Labor website at www.dol.gov or United States Equal Employment Opportunity Commission at www.eeoc.gov.

Civil Rights Act of 1964 and Title VII

The Civil Rights Act of 1964 and Title VII are extremely important and are two of the strongest U.S. civil rights laws affecting employment. These laws were introduced with the intent of reducing and eliminating discrimination in the workplace based upon specific elements or protected classes.

Below are some key points about these laws that influence discriminatory practices in the workplace:

- Title VII of the Civil Rights Act of 1964 prohibits employment discrimination based on race, color, religion, sex or national origin;

- Discrimination under this Act and related employment Acts (GINA, ADA, and ADEA) includes, but is not limited to, the following in employment actions:

  a. Hiring and firing.
  b. Employment testing
  c. Recruiting ads
  d. Promotions

    e. Recruiting practices
    f. Compensation
    g. Benefits
    h. Retirement
    i. Disability leave
    j. Layoffs

- Other prohibited acts in the course of employment include:

    a. Harassment on the basis of race, color, religion, sex, national origin, disability, genetic information or age.
    b. Retaliation for filing a charge of discrimination, participating in an investigation or opposing/not participating in discriminatory practices.
    c. Employment decisions based upon stereotypes.

For more information about the Civil Rights Act of 1964 and Title VII, please visit the Equal Employment Opportunity Commission's website at www.eeoc.gov and The National Archive's website at www.archives.gov/education/lessons/civil-rights-act/.

Age Discrimination in Employment Act of 1967 (ADEA)

- The Age Discrimination in Employment Act of 1967 was put into effect to protect applicants and employees, 40 years of age and older, from discrimination in the workplace based upon their age.

- The ADEA applies to employers with 20 or more employees. This includes state, local and federal governments, employment agencies and labor organizations.

- The ADEA makes it unlawful to discriminate against a person because of his/her age with respect to any condition or element of their employment including such facets as hiring, firing, layoffs, training, compensation and benefits.

- The ADEA makes it unlawful to retaliate against an individual for actions such as not-engaging in or opposing discriminatory employment practices, whether based upon age, filing or participating in an age discrimination complaint or for participating in an investigation under the ADEA.

- During the course of a settlement, or with terms of termination or a layoff, an employer is entitled to ask an employee to waive their rights or claims under the ADEA. There are, though, specific elements that must be met for a waiver of these rights to be considered valid. Below are listed the main requirements:

  a. The waiver must be in writing and must be clear and understandable.
  b. It must clearly and specifically refer to ADEA rights or claims.
  c. It must not waive the person's future rights or claims.
  d. It must be in exchange for valuable consideration (something in return, i.e., compensation, benefits,) It must advise the person that they have the right to consult an attorney before signing the waiver.
  e. It must provide that the person has at least 21 days to consider the agreement and at least 7 days to revoke the agreement after signing it.

For more information about the Age Discrimination in Employment Act of 1967, please visit the Equal Employment Opportunity Commission's website at www.eeoc.gov.

Title II of the Genetic Information Nondiscrimination Act of 2008(GINA)

November 21, 2009, saw the introduction of laws prohibiting discrimination against people seeking or engaged in employment, as based upon their genetic information.

Below are some key highlights of the Act:

- The Equal Employment Opportunity Commission is responsible for enforcing the provisions of Title II of GINA.

- The concept of "genetic information" refers to any information about a person's genetic tests and the genetic tests of family members. It also includes information related to a person's medical history of conditions, disorders or diseases.

- Title II of the Genetic Information Nondiscrimination Act makes it illegal to discriminate against applicants for employment or employees based upon genetic information. Thus, it prohibits the use of genetic information when an employer makes decisions related to employment. It also limits the subsequent disclosure of the genetic information.

- Discrimination in employment under Title II of GINA includes, but is not limited to, employment actions such as hiring, firing, promotions, training, benefits, compensation and layoffs.

- Title II of GINA also makes it illegal for an employer to harass (i.e., offensive remarks or comments about an employee based upon their genetic information), retaliate, demote or fire and employee due to the employee making a complaint of discrimination based upon genetic information.

For more information about Title II of the Genetic Information Nondiscrimination Act of 2008, please visit the EEOC's website at www.eeoc.gov.

Resources for Military Reservists

There are two significant sets of legislation of which military personnel in the private sector should be aware. These are the Uniformed Services Employment and Reemployment Rights Act of 1994 (USERRA) and Family and Medical Leave Act (FMLA). Below is an overview of how these two pieces of legislation affect reservists:

Uniformed Services Employment and Reemployment Act of 1994 (USERRA)

- Applies to all public and private employers in the United States. Includes local, state and federal governments. There is no company size requirement.

- Allows employees to participate in military service.

- Protects individuals from discrimination based upon their service.

- Allows for the reinstatement of employee benefits.

- Provides for reinstatement to their job following military service. Below is a time table for return to work:

  a. If 1-30 days of service, report on the next scheduled work day.
  b. If 31-180 days of service, apply within 14 days following the completion of service.
  c. If 181 or more days of service, apply within 90 days following the completion of service.

- Individuals seeking reemployment under USERRA need to be aware of the following:

  a. You must provide your employer with advance notice of your service.
  b. You must return to work according to the requirements of USERRA.
  c. You were not separated from service due to disqualifying discharge, other than honorable conditions.

For more information about USERRA, please visit the U.S. Department of Labor's website at www.dol.gov.

Family and Medical Leave Act (FMLA)

- In 2008, new benefit entitlements were added to the FMLA related to military service members.

Qualifying exigency leave under which eligible employees may take up to 12 weeks of FMLA leave for reasons related to the call to active duty of covered service member spouses, children or parent.

Military caregiver leave, which provides employees up to 26 weeks of leave in a single 12-month period to care for a covered service member who is seriously injured or ill.

- FMLA year calculations for military caregivers begin with the first date of the caregiver leave and end after 12 months.

- The 26 weeks period of caregiver leave may be taken at once or intermittently.

- Military caregiver leave is determined per service member, per injury.

- In 2009, additional changes were made to reflect that families of service members on active duty in the regular armed services are now eligible for this type of leave if the service member is deployed on active duty in a foreign country.

- To qualify for exigency FMLA leave, there are criteria that must be met, such as:

  a. Spending time with the covered service member during breaks during deployment.
  b. Post-employment activities.
  c. Military events.
  d. Legal and financial events related to family member's active duty.
  e. Urgent school or childcare related activities.
  f. When the service member receives one or less weeks' notice of deployment.
  g. Counseling of non-FMLA covered employees or children.

For more information about eligibility, procedures and clarification of military and caregiver leaves under FMLA, please visit the U.S. Department of Labor's website at www.dol.gov.

List of Recruiting and Temporary Agencies

The following list includes a combination of some pretty well known temporary and direct placement agencies. Some are specifically engaged in the business of temporary employees, while others are more focused on placing matching individuals with companies on a direct hire basis.

It is important to note that like online job boards, there are recruiting and temporary agencies that are general (any type position) and there are others that are job or industry specific. If you are interested in working with a more specific or niche agency, I always encourage that you take the time to conduct online searches for those types of agencies.

- Account Temps   www.accounttemps.com
- Adecco   www.adecco.com
- Aerotek   www.aerotek.com
- Apple One   www.appleone.com
- Korn Ferry   www.kornferry.com
- Management Recruiters   www.mrinetwork.com
- Manpower   www.manpower.com
- Office Team   www.officeteam.com
- Olsten   www.olsten.com
- Robert Half   www.roberthalf.com
- Select   www.selectstaffing.com
- Spherion   www.spherion.com
- Volt   jobs.volt.com

List of Commonly Used Online Job Boards

The following list of online job search sites is just a brief sample of some of the most commonly utilized job search engines on the web. It is important to know that online job search sites may be general or specific to a role/job or industry (i.e., manufacturing, healthcare, services, etc.). There are also job search sites that focus on specific job levels (i.e., Vice Presidents, CFOs, other executives, etc.) and compensation ranges. If you are seeking a specific or niche type of role, conduct searches at sites that meet your needs. Several helpful sites are listed below:

www.6figurejobs.com

www.careerbuilder.com

www.careerjournal.com

www.craigslist.com

www.dice.com

www.diversityjobs.com

www.execunet.com

www.hotjobs.com

www.indeed.com

www.job.com

www.jobfox.com

www.latimes.com

www.linkedin.com

www.monster.com

www.simplyhired.com

www.theladders.com

About the Author

Dr. Carlyle W. Rogers is a career business professional with extensive experience planning and leading organizational human resources, operations, and strategy. Additionally, he has been an executive and developmental coach to many Presidents, CEOs, and Boards of Directors.

He has held a variety of senior executive roles including CAO for Sonic Electronix, Inc., VP of Human Resources for arvato digital services (a division of Bertelsmann) and Sizzler USA Restaurants, and Director of Human Resources and Legal for Gruber Systems, Inc. In addition to his corporate experience, he provided human resources and general business consulting services to a variety of companies in many industries.

Dr. Rogers possesses a BA in Psychology, MS in Family and Consumer Science with a specialization in Family Studies, PsyD in Psychology, and Juris Doctor. Additionally, he is a certified interrogator and interviewer. He maintains membership with the American Bar Association, American Psychological Association, California Psychological Association, Society for Human Resources Management, and Reid Institute of Trained Investigators.

Outside of work, Dr. Rogers spends his time in his primary job... husband to wife Iris and father to daughters Mya and Jeanelle.

.

www.ingramcontent.com/pod-product-compliance
Lightning Source LLC
Chambersburg PA
CBHW051543170526
45165CB00002B/854